LEVEL F

# STRATEGIES FOR SUCCESS in Writing

Estelle Kleinman

*Strategies for Success in Writing — Level F*

ISBN 0-7398-1049-9

Copyright © 2000 Steck-Vaughn Company.
All rights reserved. No part of this book may be reproduced or utilized in any form or by any means, electronic or mechanical, including photocopying, recording, or by any information storage and retrieval system, without permission in writing from the publisher. Inquiries should be addressed to: Copyright Permissions, Steck-Vaughn Company, P.O. Box 26015, Austin, TX 78755. Printed in the United States.

Published by © Steck-Vaughn/Berrent Publications, a division of Steck-Vaughn Company.

1 2 3 4 5 6 7 8 9 HG 04 03 02 01 00 99

## Credits

**Project Editor:** Amy Losi

**Executive Editor:** Karen Bischoff

**Editor:** Debra Tursi

**Design Director:** Steven Coleman

**Design and Layout:** Jan Jarvis, *Michael William Printery*

**Electronic Production Specialist:** Jean-Paul Vest

**Illustration:** Jack Kershner, *Lancelot Art*

# Table of Contents

# Preface

Our society cannot work well if people cannot read, write, or do math. Testing is one way that teachers can find out how well you are learning these skills. It is the way we measure both your success as a learner and our success as teachers.

The materials in this book have been carefully prepared to help you learn the skills you will need to do well on tests. You will become aware of your strengths and weaknesses, and you can practice the skills that give you trouble.

This book also provides you with test-taking strategies. These strategies will give you that extra edge you need to do well on tests. Our job is to give you the tools you need to succeed. We wish you well!

# Unit 1 Prewriting Strategies

## CHAPTER One

### Getting Started

You may believe that after leaving school, you will not need to write. You may not write the same types of materials as you do now; however, you will be doing some form of writing.

For some students, writing is a painful task. It is something they try not to do whenever possible. These students are not alone. Many people are unsure of their writing ability.

All writers try to produce quality writing. It is difficult to decide what to say, how to say it, and how to make it grammatically correct. Professional writers do not create an article, a story, or a book all by themselves. They have people who read what they have written, offering suggestions and advice. They have editors, too, who help them by editing and proofreading their work. So, if you experience difficulty while writing, you are not alone. You are in the company of some of the world's best writers.

We can compare writing to the sport of bowling. In bowling, you take the ball, focus on the pins, approach the line, and send the ball down the lane. If you are very good, or very lucky, you may knock down all the pins and score a strike. But more than likely, you will leave pins standing. You then get another chance to knock down the remaining pins. Unfortunately, even with this second chance, you may leave some pins standing. The game goes on and you repeat the process over and over again.

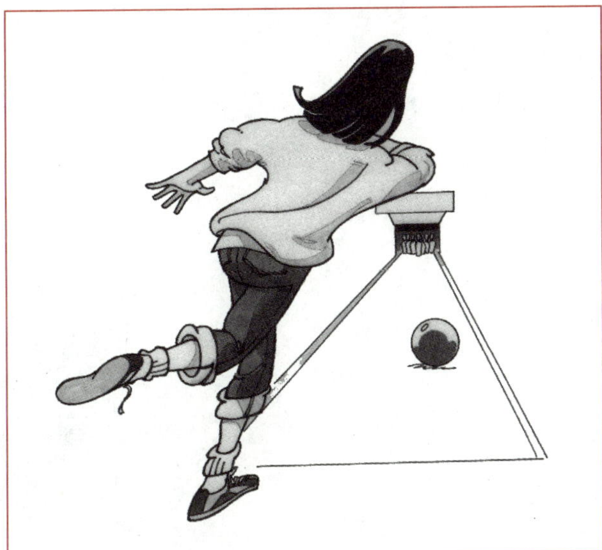

In writing, you take your pen or pencil, focus on and think about your assignment, approach your task by organizing your ideas, and begin to write. As in bowling, you get a second chance to improve your work. You write your first draft, followed by a chance to rewrite, and then you revise and edit your work.

Although few bowlers ever bowl a perfect game, they keep trying to perfect their skills to achieve that goal. As a writer, you may not produce the perfect paper. However, your work will improve with continued practice and revisions.

## The Four Types of Writing

It may seem like there are thousands of different kinds of writing. There are science fiction books, social studies textbooks, instructions on how to play a game, newspaper articles, advertisements, writing on cereal boxes, and letters. These may seem to have nothing in common, yet there are really only four types of writing: narrative, informational, persuasive/argumentative, and everyday.

- The first thing you need to know is what you are writing. Often your teacher decides this for you. You are assigned to write a story or a lab report or an essay. However, you also write things that you are not assigned: a letter to a friend, a note to your parent, a list of what you want for your birthday.
- What you write will determine the form your writing will take. For instance, you would not write a story in the same way you would write a note to your parent. Not only would they look different, but the writing would be different. The writing in a story describes things, and it is more creative. It is meant to be read by a lot of different people. The writing in a note is short and to the point. It usually includes facts and is read by one person, or maybe a few specific people.

Each type of writing—narrative, informational, persuasive/argumentative, everyday—has its own general form and style. Although the pieces of writing are different within a category, the writing still follows the basic rules of that category.

## Narrative Text

Narrative text tells a story. Stories can retell actual events, such as biographies, or they can be completely fictional or imaginary, such as a science fiction novel. They are called narrative texts because they narrate something; they tell the story of a real or made-up event.

All narrative texts have the same four basic parts: characters (people, animals, and/or fictional creatures), setting (when and where the story takes place), plot (events that happen), and a theme (the message).

1. List three specific narrative texts and the reasons they are narratives.

## Informational Text

Informational text teaches you something. You read and write a lot of informational text while in school. Textbooks fall in this category, as well as the reports that you write. They are called informational texts because they provide information on specific topics.

Informational texts contain many facts. Before starting this type of writing you must do research.

2. List three specific informational texts (other than school textbooks) and explain why they are informational.

## Persuasive/Argumentative Text

Persuasive/argumentative text is written in the hopes of bringing about change. The writer uses argument, reason, facts, and opinion to try to persuade the reader(s) to do something or to think a certain way. Think of persuasive/argumentative text as making a case to a jury. Naturally, you would try as hard as you could to make them believe your side of the case. The more persuasive your case, the better your chance that the jury will agree with your position.

Persuasive/argumentative texts do three basic things: They ask you to use logic by giving you facts and reasons; they appeal to your emotions by using descriptions and colorful language to get you to feel something; and they try to impress you with the words of experts.

**3.** List three specific persuasive/argumentative texts and explain why they belong in this category.

## Everyday Text

Everyday text is useful. The purpose of everyday text is to give you concise information about something that you need to do or understand. Some examples of this useful type of writing are as follows: a road sign, a list of rules, a form, a television guide, a menu, and a recipe. These are called everyday texts because they are things that you read everyday.

Everyday texts always have a message to get across. They are straightforward and to the point, and contain very little, if any, extra detail.

**4.** List three everyday texts not mentioned above and the reasons why they belong in this category.

## Forms of Writing

Writing can take many forms. It can be a simple note you write to yourself; it can be a letter to a friend; it can be a report for school; or it can be an article for the school newspaper. After high school, your writing may include office memos, business reports, or instructions on how to do something. Each form of writing has its own style. Letters, in particular, have a special style that you should always follow.

## Friendly Letter

When you write to your family or close friends, you are writing a friendly letter. Even though the subject will vary from letter to letter, the form should remain the same. On some writing tests, you may be asked questions about the parts of a letter, how it is punctuated, or which words are capitalized.

### Friendly Letter

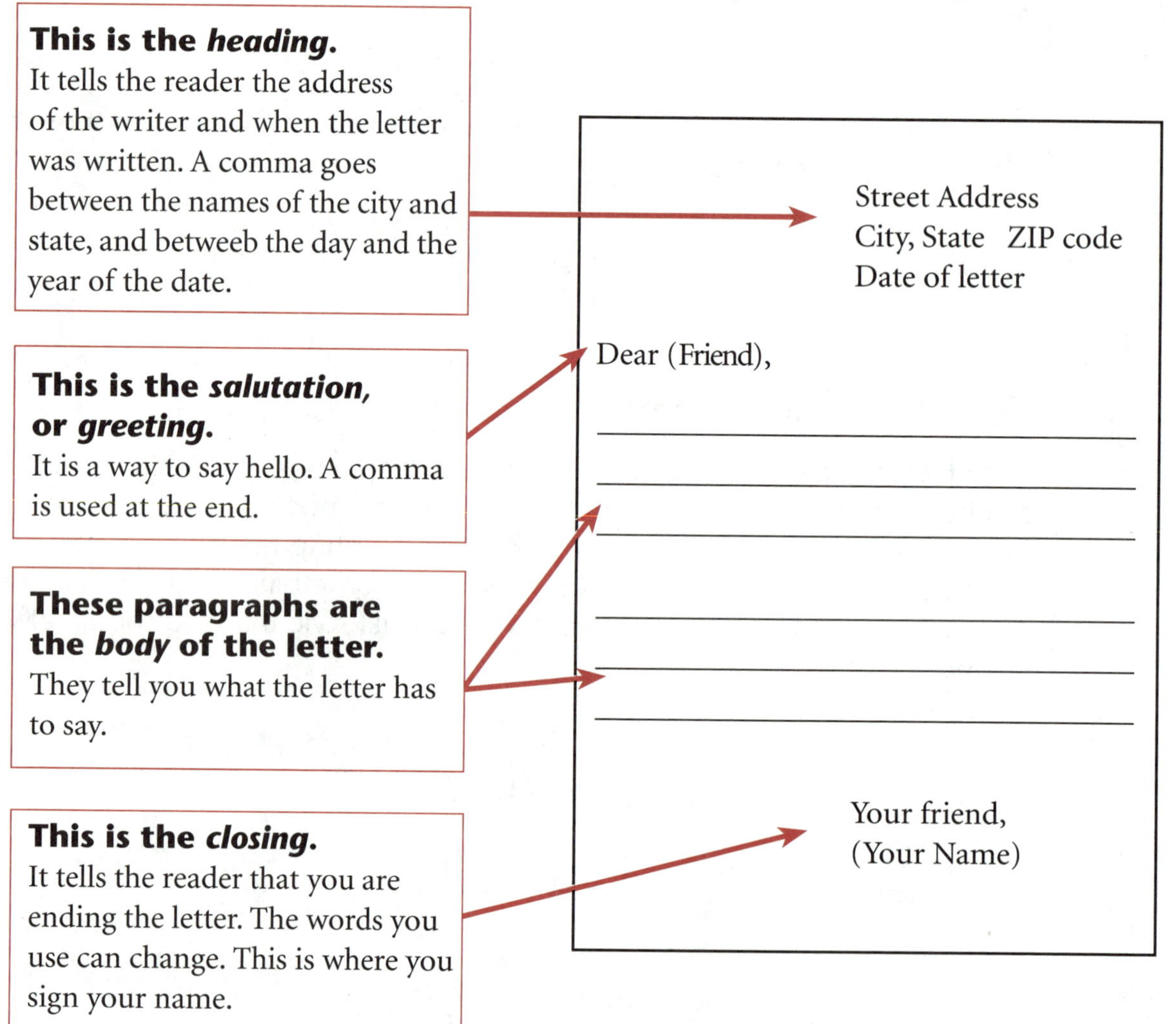

# Address Abbreviations

Here is how you can shorten some common address words:

| Street Name | Abbreviation | Street Name | Abbreviation |
|---|---|---|---|
| Avenue | Ave. | Boulevard | Blvd. |
| Court | Ct. | Drive | Dr. |
| Lane | Ln. | Place | Pl. |
| Road | Rd. | Street | St. |

When you shorten, or *abbreviate*, the names of states in the United States, there are two forms you can use. The standard abbreviation contains two or more letters and is followed by a period. The post office has its own way to abbreviate state names. Postal abbreviations have only two letters. Both letters are capitalized and there is no period. Below is a chart showing the standard and postal abbreviations for the United States.

| State | Standard | Postal | State | Standard | Postal | State | Standard | Postal |
|---|---|---|---|---|---|---|---|---|
| Alabama | Ala. | AL | Kentucky | Ky. | KY | Oklahoma | Okla. | OK |
| Alaska | | AK | Louisiana | La. | LA | Oregon | Ore. | OR |
| American Samoa | | AS | Maine | Me. | ME | Pennsylvania | Penn. | PA |
| Arizona | Ariz. | AZ | Maryland | Md. | MD | Puerto Rico | P.R. | PR |
| Arkansas | Ark. | AR | Massachusetts | Mass. | MA | Rhode Island | R.I. | RI |
| California | Calif. | CA | Michigan | Mich. | MI | South Carolina | S.C. | SC |
| Colorado | Colo. | CO | Minnesota | Minn. | MN | South Dakota | S.Dak. | SD |
| Connecticut | Conn. | CT | Mississippi | Miss. | MS | Tennessee | Tenn. | TN |
| Delaware | Del. | DE | Missouri | Mo. | MO | Texas | Tex. | TX |
| Florida | Fla. | FL | Montana | Mont. | MT | Utah | | UT |
| Georgia | Ga. | GA | Nebraska | Nebr. | NE | Vermont | Vt. | VT |
| Guam | | GU | Nevada | Nev. | NV | Virginia | Va. | VA |
| Hawaii | | HI | New Hampshire | N.H. | NH | Virgin Islands | V.I. | VI |
| Idaho | Ida. | ID | New Jersey | N.J. | NJ | Washington | Wash. | WA |
| Illinois | Ill. | IL | New Mexico | N.Mex. | NM | Washington, D.C. | D.C. | DC |
| Indiana | Ind. | IN | New York | N.Y. | NY | West Virginia | W.Va. | WV |
| Iowa | Ia. | IA | North Carolina | N.C. | NC | Wisconsin | Wis. | WI |
| Kansas | Kans. | KS | North Dakota | N.Dak. | ND | Wyoming | Wyo. | WY |
| | | | Ohio | | OH | | | |

**Note:** There are no standard abbreviations for Alaska, American Samoa, Guam, Hawaii, Ohio, and Utah.

Standard abbreviations can be used in the address in the heading of a friendly letter. Postal abbreviations are used on envelopes.

Let us look at how we address the envelope for a friendly letter. On the upper left-hand side of the envelope, you should put your name and address. At about the center of the envelope, put the name and address of the person who will receive the letter. Here is a sample for you to see.

Ms. Eve Dupree
617 Fulton Avenue
Talmoon, MN 56637

Mr. Jack Montego
4201 Willow Drive
Lake Placid, NY 12946

**5.** Write a short letter to a friend, address an envelope, and mail your letter.

## Business Letter

If you have not yet done so, you will surely need to write a business letter at some time. Some uses for these letters are to request information, to discuss or complain about a product or service, and to apply for a job. Business letters are more formal than friendly letters, and they are different in form.

A business letter includes a heading, a salutation, the body, and a closing. Unlike a friendly letter, a business letter also includes an inside address. The inside address gives the name and address of the person receiving the letter. Here is an example of an inside address:

Mr. Wilson Tuttle, Sales Manager
Western Sporting Goods Company
5609 North Canal Street
Chicago, IL 66780

## Business Letter

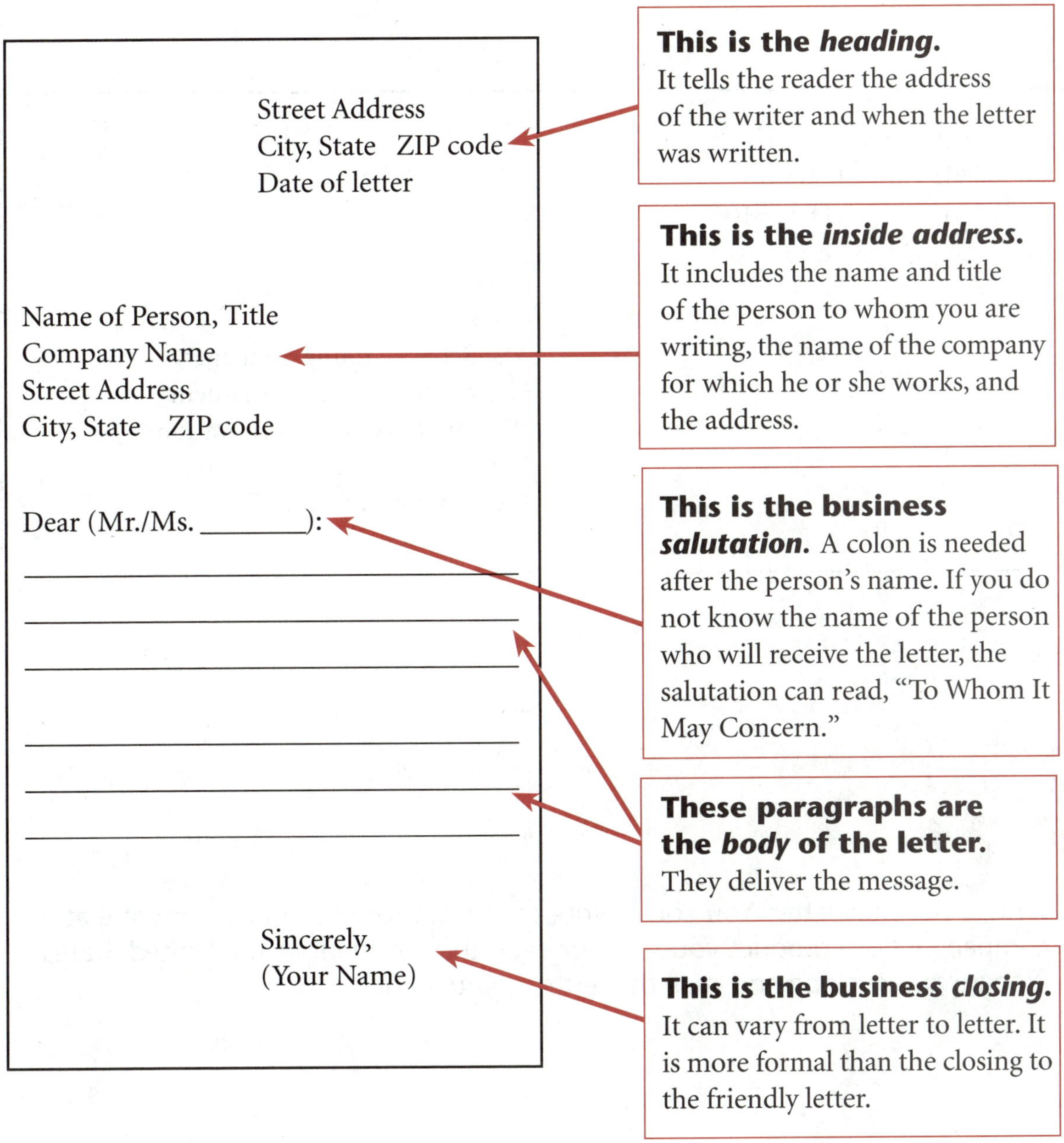

Street Address
City, State ZIP code
Date of letter

Name of Person, Title
Company Name
Street Address
City, State ZIP code

Dear (Mr./Ms. ________):

Sincerely,
(Your Name)

**This is the *heading*.** It tells the reader the address of the writer and when the letter was written.

**This is the *inside address*.** It includes the name and title of the person to whom you are writing, the name of the company for which he or she works, and the address.

**This is the business *salutation*.** A colon is needed after the person's name. If you do not know the name of the person who will receive the letter, the salutation can read, "To Whom It May Concern."

**These paragraphs are the *body* of the letter.** They deliver the message.

**This is the business *closing*.** It can vary from letter to letter. It is more formal than the closing to the friendly letter.

It is usually not appropriate to use abbreviations in business letters. However, there are two exceptions. You should use the abbreviation *Mr.* or *Ms.* before a person's name. You can also use the dollar sign ($) indicating the cost of an item. If you cannot type your letter, be sure that your handwriting is legible and that you print your name underneath your signature.

The envelopes for a business and a friendly letter are similar. Your name and address should appear in the upper left-hand corner of the envelope. The center of the envelope should have the name of the person you are writing to, followed by his or her business title, if there is one. (If you do not have a person's name, you can leave this off.) On the next line, put the company name. This is followed by the company address. Here is a sample business envelope:

Mr. Paul Wilson
90802 Parkside Drive
Morrisville, MO 65710

Ms. Rebecca Young, Manager
Customer Service Department
Wheeler & Wilson Corporation
3617 Commerce Boulevard
Indianapolis, IN 46241

**6.** Write a business letter. You could write to the author of a book, someone at a company whose product you own, or even the President of the United States. Prepare an envelope and mail the letter, if you want.

## ADDRESS ABBREVIATIONS

| Provinces | Standard | Postal |
|---|---|---|
| Alberta | Alta. | AB |
| British Columbia | B.C. | BC |
| Manitoba | Man. | MB |
| New Brunswick | N.B. | NB |
| Newfoundland | Nfld. | NF |
| Northwest Territories | N.W. Terr. | NT |
| Nova Scotia | N.S. | NS |
| Ontario | Ont. | ON |
| Prince Edward Island | P.E.I. | PE |
| Quebec | Que. | PQ or QC |
| Saskatchewan | Sask. | SK |
| Yukon Territory | Yukon Terr. | YT |

**7.** Imagine that you are planning a trip to some part of Canada. You want to know what to see, where to stay, what to wear, as well as get a map of the area. Write a letter asking for information so you can plan your trip carefully. You can find out the addresses of tourist offices in the different provinces or territories on your own, or use the following address:

Tourism Canada
Industry, Science & Technology Canada
235 Queen Street
Ottawa, ON  K1A 0H5

(The postal codes for Canada are different from those for the United States. The Canadian codes contain both letters and numbers. The United States codes are only numbers.)

## Notes

When you want to write something short and informal, you can write a note. A note is a quick message that you write to your family and friends. A note can be used to tell something to a friend, to tell your parents where you're going, or even to remind yourself to do something. This is one of the most common forms of writing.

A business note is called a memo. Memos are brief and to the point, and usually give information or mention something that needs to be done.

A business memo might look like this:

To: Barry Palma
From: Allan O'Malley
Re: Sales Meeting
Date: May 5, 1998

Arrangements have been made for you to attend the regional sales meeting in New Orleans from May 11 to 13. Jean Smith has made your hotel reservations and booked your flight. She'll have all the details for you on Tuesday morning. Let's meet for dinner Wednesday evening. We should go over our report before our meeting on Thursday. Call my room when you arrive. If I'm out, leave a message at the front desk, and I'll phone you when I get back.

This memo covers just the basics. A memo contains the necessary information and nothing extra.

## Other Forms of Writing

Writing can take many other forms. There are books, plays, invitations, school reports, class notes, catalogs, menus, and so on. These other forms do not follow a strict form like a letter. The writer decides what form the writing should take. If your teacher assigns you a piece of writing, he or she may determine the form.

# Topics for Writing Assignments

In school, you are asked to do a lot of writing. Usually, you are given some guidelines for your writing. You may not realize it, but your writing assignments fall into four categories. These categories are as follows:

- a general topic, probably related to something you are studying
- a specific topic, again probably related to class work
- a list of specific topics to choose from
- free choice to write about anything you want

There are good and bad points about each of these categories for you, the writer. If assigned a specific topic that you are not interested in, you may find it hard to write something. The greater choice you have in your writing assignment, the more chance you have of writing about something that interests you. However, the more choice you have, the harder it is to choose a topic. It may seem as though you have so many options that you do not know where to begin.

The best strategy to follow when given a choice in writing topics is to pick something you are familiar with or something that you find interesting or fun. The more you enjoy what you are writing about, the better your writing will be. If you are confused or bored with a writing topic, your writing will reflect this.

8. **General Topic:** You are studying American history in school. Your teacher has asked you to write a report about any war in this country's past. Come up with three topics that you could write about.

9. **Specific Topic:** Come up with three specific topics that relate to something you have studied this year.

10. **List of Topics:** Pretend you are a science teacher. Come up with a list of three topics that you want your class to choose from for a paper.

11. **Free Choice:** You have to write a two-page essay about anything you want. What are three things that you would like to write about?

## Audience

Once you know what you are writing, the next step is to decide who will read what you have written. The people who will read it are your audience. If you are writing in a journal, your audience will be yourself. If you are writing a report for your teacher, he or she will be your audience. Your teacher could ask you to write a story that will be read aloud to the class. Or you could write an article for your school newspaper that could be read by everyone in the school.

Your audience will have an effect on what you write. For instance, when writing a specific homework assignment for a teacher, you assume the teacher will be the only one to read your writing. You are writing to him or her. You know that your teacher understands the topic you are writing about, so you don't explain every detail.

However, if your teacher let you write about whatever you wanted, he or she may not be familiar with the topic. For instance, if you wrote about your favorite band, your teacher might not know anything about them. You are the authority on the topic, and your writing will explain the information to your teacher.

If you had to write an article for a newspaper, you would be writing to a large audience. Before you write anything, you would need to think about what those people want to know.

Let's say your family decides to hold a yard sale. You want to advertise the event, so you decide to put up signs around the neighborhood. These signs are for a large audience—your whole neighborhood. Think about what you want to tell them. You want to announce the date, time, place, and the kinds of items you will be selling. You should include a reason why your neighbors would want to attend the sale.

## Audience Concept Map

The Audience Concept Map can help you picture the different types of audiences. It can also help you understand how your writing is influenced by the audience who will read it.

**Family and Friends:** The people you know the best fill the center audience. This includes your family and very close friends. What you write to them is usually in a chatty and less formal style.

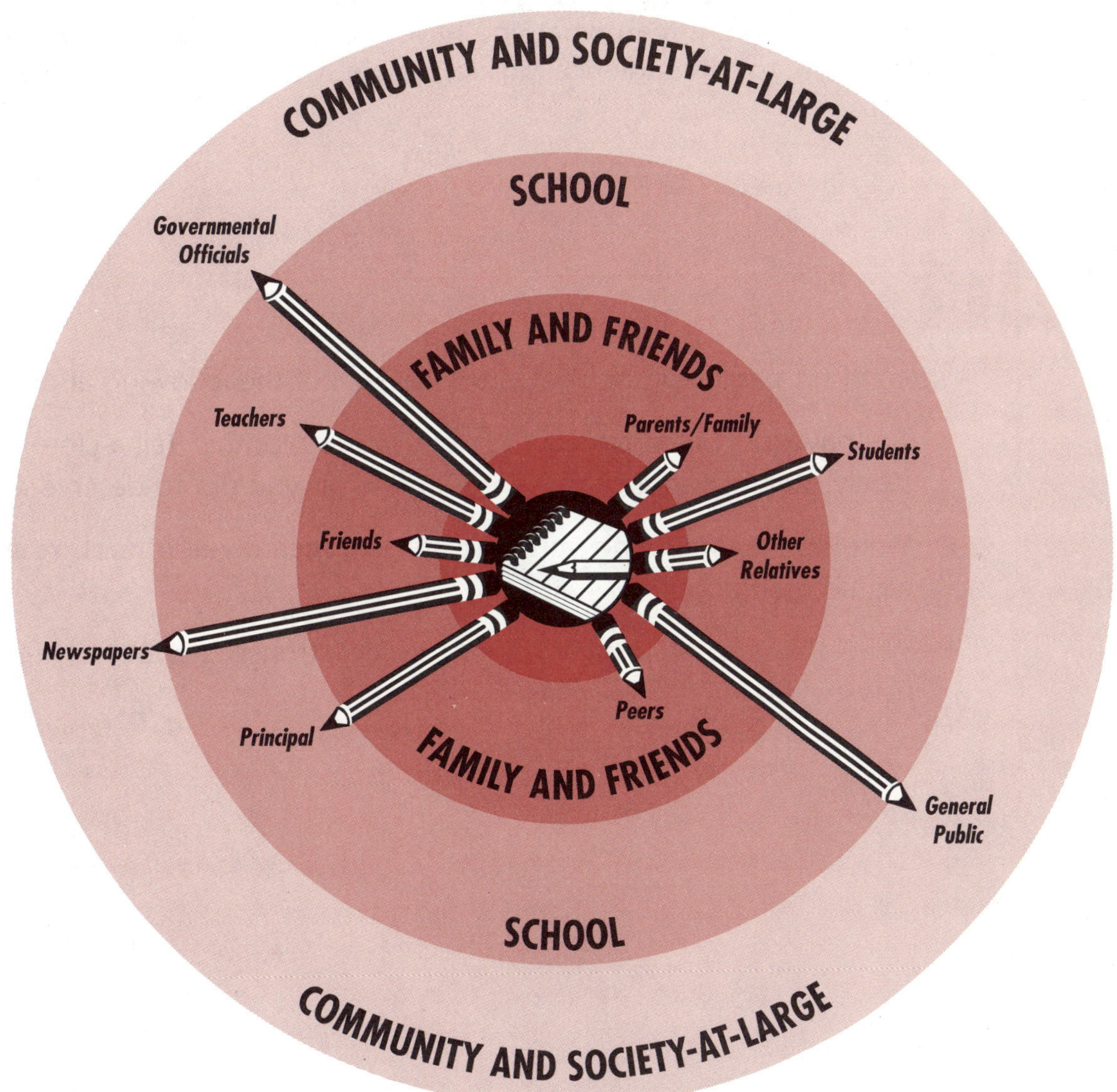

**School:** This includes all of the people you write for when you are in school. Most of the writing you do for this audience is to fulfill class assignments. Your writing is more formal than when you write to friends or family. You need to pay attention to content, structure, and technical accuracy when writing for this audience.

Included in the school audience are people who may not know you well, such as the principal. When you write to them, it can be to express your views on something of interest to you. You need to give careful consideration to your writing. If it is not well constructed and not correctly worded, it may not receive much attention.

**Community/Society-at-Large:** This is the largest audience. It is made up of anyone who might read what you have written. Book authors and newspaper reporters write to this audience. So do people who write advertisements and road signs.

**12.** Write a short paragraph or brief letter for each of the following audiences:

- You have just been named "Student of the Month." Tell a close friend or family member about this award, and what you did to deserve it.
- Write about something you have studied recently at school. Your teacher will be grading it.
- Write about an issue or problem you feel strongly about for your school newspaper.

# Getting Organized

Before a building can be built, a blueprint or plan has to be drawn. The same idea applies to writing. You have to plan before you write. Prewriting is a blueprint for good writing and will help you decide on the form your writing will take. You need to know your purpose for writing and the audience who will read what you have written. All of this has to be planned before you put the first words on paper. After that, you can concentrate on what you want to say.

Once you know your purpose, audience, and form, you need to organize your thoughts and ideas. You want your writing to flow smoothly and make sense. That way, your audience will better understand what you have to say. There is no one best way to organize information, and there are different ways to get started.

## Organizing Narrative Writing

When writing a story, you must remember to include four basic things: characters (people, animals, and/or fictional creatures), setting (when and where the story takes place), plot (events that happen), and a theme (the message). When organizing your writing, you should outline what these things are going to be. Remember, an outline is only a guideline to help you write. You do not need to stick to it. Sometimes a story changes as you start writing because better ideas come to mind.

The most important part of any story is the plot. This is the series of events that make up the center of the story. When outlining a story, it may be easier to start with the plot. Once you have the plot, the characters, setting, and theme usually fall into place.

## Story Model

This outlining technique will help you organize your story in the following way:

**1.** After the beginning or exposition of the story, a problem occurs.

**2.** Then there is a series of events that leads to a climax, the most important point in the story, or a solution.

**3.** After the problem is solved, there is an ending or a resolution.

When outlining the model it, should look something like this:

### Story Model

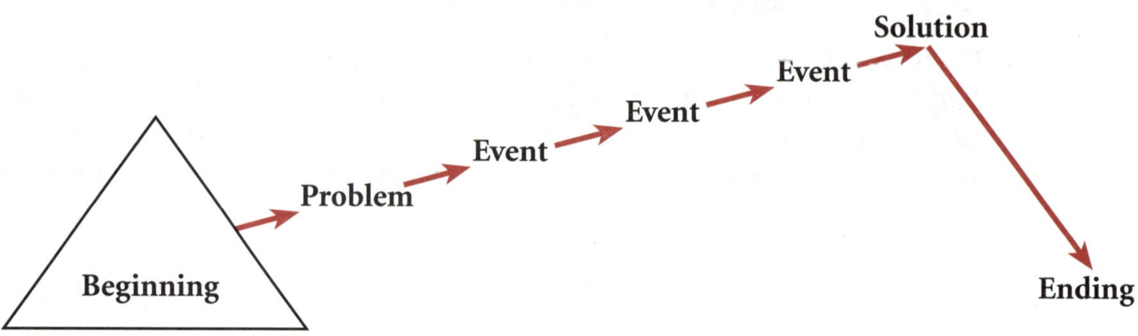


This is just a form for you to follow. Of course, your story may have more or fewer events. It may also have more than one problem to be solved.

**1.** Come up with an idea for a story. The story can be about anything you want. It can be a fairy tale, science fiction, a mystery, or a story based on your life. Create a story model of your plot, following the outline given above. Remember, this is just an outline. You do not need to fill in all the details, just the major events. (A story suggestion: Your parents have gone away for the weekend. You and your younger brother/sister are home alone. Something bad happens.)

## Story Map

A story map is a great way to outline the key parts of a narrative story. This map will help you highlight the main parts of your story. You can show the beginning, middle, and ending of your story. Another way is to show the story's setting, characters, problem, and solution.

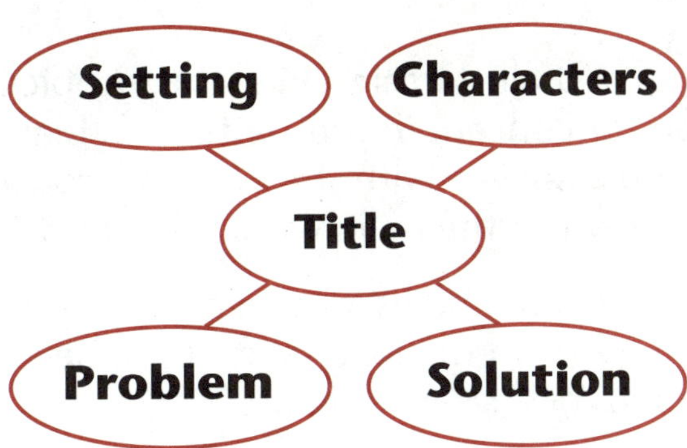

# Organizing Informational, Persuasive/ Argumentative, and Everyday Writing

The following strategies can be used for any of the other three forms of writing: informational, persuasive/argumentative, and everyday. These strategies are interchangeable. There are no hard-and-fast rules as to which strategy to use with each kind of text. When organizing your writing, use whichever strategy works best for you.

## Mapping

Mapping is a way of brainstorming ideas on a topic before writing. You start with a general word or concept in the center of a blank paper. Then you write other words that you associate with that word or concept on the page. Circle them and connect them to the main word with lines.

The mapping strategy can be used with any form of writing. However, this is a good way to organize informational text. It is a helpful strategy to use when writing a social studies or a science report.

When you start to make a map, no matter what the topic, you will be surprised at how many things you can come up with. You will probably find that you know much more about a topic than you thought.

Remember, it isn't practical to include everything from your map in your writing. You can choose to write about the things in only one part of the map. This will make your writing more focused. Your attention will be on a limited amount of information, rather than on too many ideas. Shown on the following page is a map that was used to organize ideas for a report on food. The person who wrote the report on food chose to concentrate on fast foods only.

## Mapping

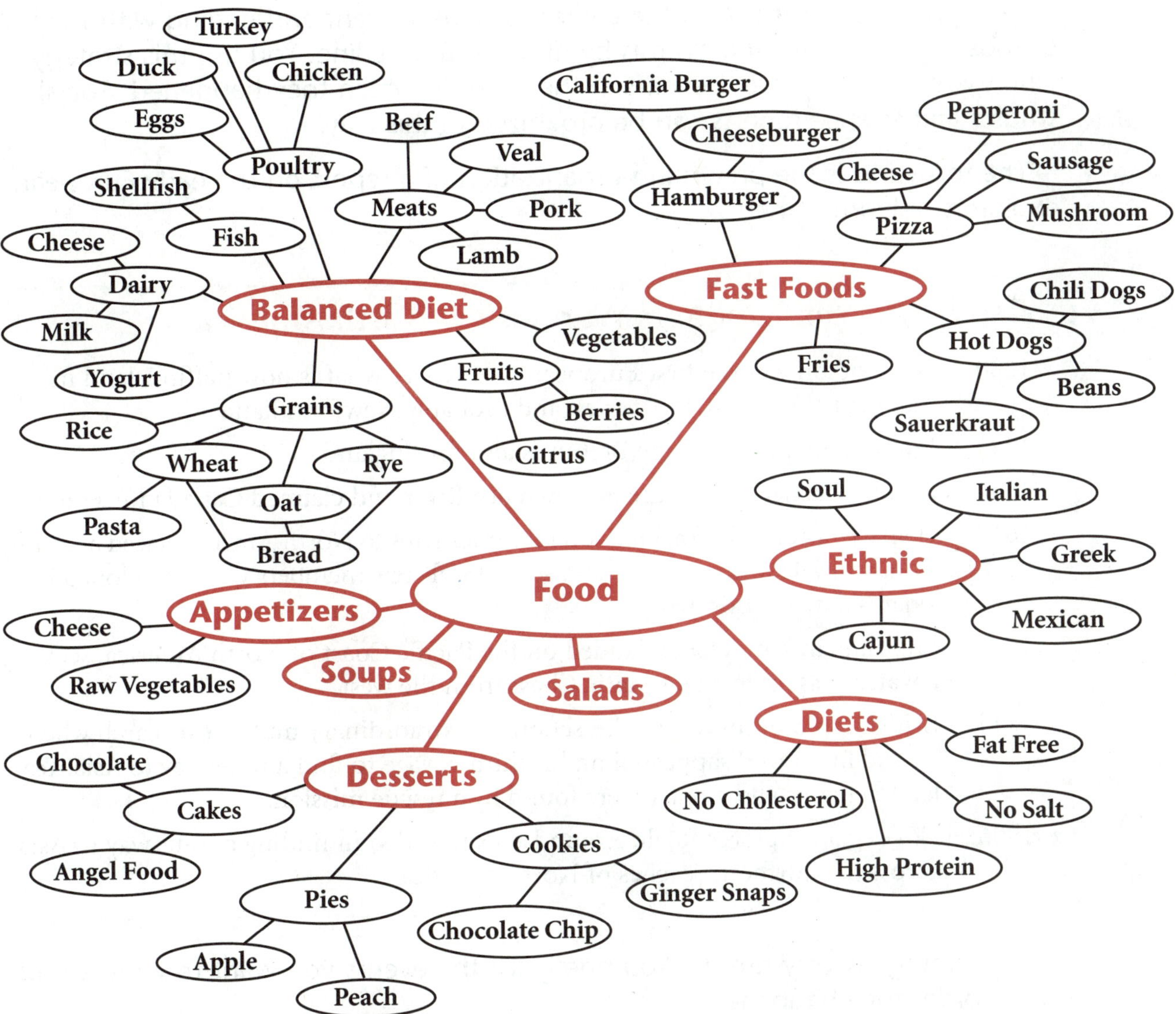


## YOUR Turn

**2.** Choose a topic from your science or social studies book. Brainstorm to create a map showing what you know about the topic. Write down the ideas as they come into your mind. Your map will start to take shape as you keep adding ideas.

## Chronological Order

Chronological order means you organize events according to the time or date they happened, starting with the earliest or oldest event and ending with the last or most recent. Often you do this by drawing a time line. You use this strategy when you want to present events in the order in which they happened. Social studies and science reports can be organized in this way.

The following is the prewriting organization of a report on the early European explorers of North America.

### Early European Explorers Who Visited North America

1000 Leif Ericson was the first European to discover what is now Baffin Island in Canada's Northwest Territories, and probably Newfoundland.

1497 John Cabot claimed Cape Breton Island for England.

1534 Jacques Cartier named the St. Lawrence River and claimed Canada for France.

1610 Henry Hudson, after making several earlier trips to North America, faced a mutiny by his crew. Hudson, his son, and seven loyal crew members were abandoned in what is now Hudson Bay.

1778 Englishman James Cook landed on the Pacific Coast of North America, seeking a water passage to the Atlantic Coast from the west.

1845 British explorer John Franklin set off an extraordinary multi-year search when he and his crew disappeared on his third voyage to find a waterway to Asia. Years later, remains and a diary were found by a rescue mission.

1906 Norwegian explorer Roald Amundsen succeeded in finding a waterway to Asia across the northern reaches of North America.

This strategy is very simple. You briefly list the events you want to write about in the order they happened.

**3.** Organize some information in chronological order. You can do this with a topic you studied in school, or pick your own topic.

## Sequential Order

Sequential order is similar to chronological order. It means to organize steps or events in a sequence, starting with the first step and ending with the last. You use this strategy when something must be written in a certain order. This is especially useful when organizing everyday text. For instance, a recipe or directions for how to make something must be written in a certain order.

Here are the basic directions for dying fabric using the batik method.

1. Get materials needed.
2. Put dye into bowls.
3. Melt wax.
4. Paint designs on the cloth with melted wax.
5. Dip fabric in dye.
6. Dry fabric.
7. Put fabric between layers of paper towels.
8. Iron fabric.

Note how brief the steps are. This is not the complete instructions for the batik method; rather, it is just an outline of the basic steps. When writing actual directions, you would fill in the steps with the details.

**4.** Organize a task in a sequential order. It can be something you do often, such as making a bed or logging onto the Internet. Or it can be a task you do only once in a while, such as baking a cake or building a model.

## Cause-and-Effect Organizer

Another helpful way to organize informational reports is by cause and effect. This also works well for organizing persuasive/argumentative writing. With this strategy, you consider how one thing can lead to another.

Here is an example of a cause-and-effect organizer that you might create for a paper about why smoking is bad for your health.

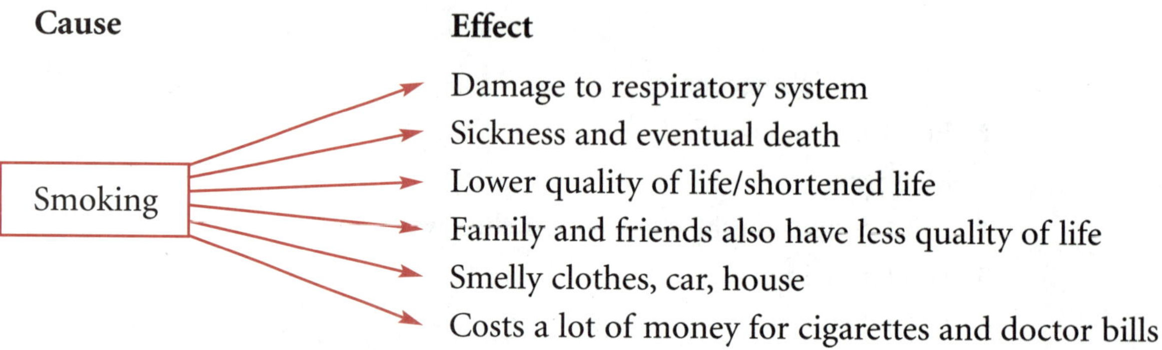


To create this organizer, you start with a cause, in this case, smoking. Then list all the effects, or things that can happen because of the cause. This organizer is good for persuasive/argumentative writing because it can help you come up with a lot of arguments to support your case.

Another use of the cause-and-effect organizer is to develop writing assignments for literature topics. To illustrate how this can help organize an English paper, you could use this method to show how a character's actions (cause) result in specific events (effect). The reverse holds true, as well. Events in a story can cause characters to act in certain ways. For instance, in Shakespeare's play *Romeo and Juliet*, the feud between the families causes the characters to react the way they do, bringing about the tragedy of the "star-crossed lovers."

**5.** Use a cause-and-effect organizer to gather your thoughts on any topic or issue. Possible topics to use as causes are as follows: the actions of a character in a book you are reading, the discovery of electricity, or the wearing of uniforms in school.

## Pro/Con Model

Another strategy that can aid you in organizing ideas for persuasive/argumentative text is the pro/con model. This strategy helps you to think carefully about an issue. Before you jump to a conclusion or rush to take a position, you need to weigh the facts carefully. You do not want to write something that you will later regret. This organizer will enable you to see how some facts outweigh others.

For the pro/con model, picture a balance scale.

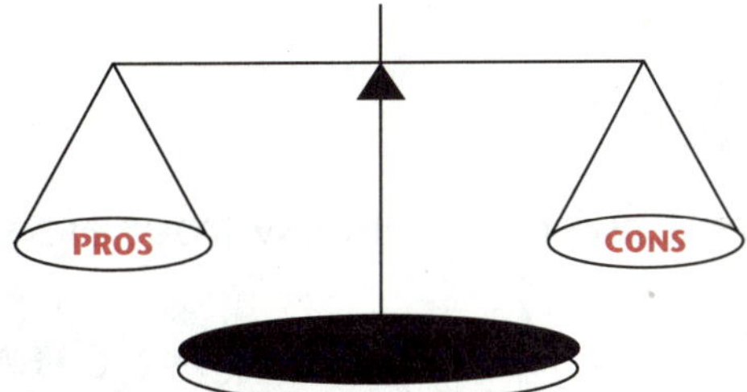


Let's say you have to write a report on recycling. You are asked to take a side, either for or against recycling. Before you write anything, you could use a pro/con chart to organize your ideas.

| PRO | CON |
|---|---|
| Less garbage in landfills | Store more garbage in homes |
| Reusing materials instead of creating more garbage | Takes time to clean & sort recyclables |
| Saves money | There's no immediate feedback for your effort |

You place the reasons supporting a position in the "Pro" column and the reasons against the position in the "Con" column. Then you can weigh both sides and decide which side you agree with.

**6.** Use a pro/con chart to gather your thoughts on any issue. Possible topics are as follows: opening a fast-food restaurant in your community, banning certain types of music, or cutting down rain forests.

## Comparison/Contrast Models

Another way to organize your ideas is to use a comparison/contrast model. This is a valuable tool when you are asked to describe how two things are similar (comparison) and/or how two things are different (contrast). These terms are often used together, or only the word "comparison" may be used to indicate how things are similar and different.

On tests or for assignments, it is very important to read the directions carefully. If you are asked to tell how things are similar as well as different, then you must do both to correctly answer the question.

## Comparison Model

Let's say you were asked to tell how frogs are similar to salamanders.

| FROGS | SALAMANDERS |
|---|---|
| Amphibians | Amphibians |
| Young (larvae) are not like adults | Young (larvae) are not like adults |
| Four-toed front feet | Four-toed front feet |
| Five-toed hind feet | Five-toed hind feet |
| Teeth | Teeth |
| Functional eyes | Functional eyes |
| Meat eaters | Meat eaters |

## Contrast Model

Here are some of the ways that frogs and salamanders are different.

| FROGS | SALAMANDERS |
|---|---|
| Legs used for jumping and swimming | Legs used for walking |
| Rid themselves of long tails | Keep long tails |
| Mostly external fertilization | Mostly internal fertilization |
| Hind legs face away from head | Hind legs face toward head |
| Teeth usually on upper jaw and on roof of mouth | Teeth on both upper and lower jaws and on roof of mouth |

## Comparison/Contrast Model

In this model, the similarities and differences are shown side by side. This is helpful when you are asked to write about both similarities and differences.

| HOW FROGS AND SALAMANDERS ARE ALIKE | HOW FROGS AND SALAMANDERS ARE DIFFERENT |
|---|---|
| Amphibians | Different skeletal structures |
| Four legs as adults | Salamanders use their legs to walk; frogs use legs for jumping and swimming |
| Different species have different colors and sizes | Salamanders have long tails; adult frogs have none |
| Gills change to lungs as adults | Salamanders have weak voices or are mute; frogs croak loudly |
| Young do not resemble their adult stage | Salamanders shed their skin; frogs don't |

**7.** Pick a topic from social studies or science and construct a comparison/contrast chart on it. If you cannot think of a topic, here are a few suggestions: two ways of doing an experiment, two geological regions, two astronomical bodies, two periods in history, two forms of government, or two important persons.

## Venn Diagram

Another way of organizing ideas for comparison and/or contrast is with a Venn diagram. The diagram shows how two things are the same and how they are different. Look at the diagram below. The outside part of each circle shows you how the two things are different. The inside section shows how the two things you are comparing are the same.

Let's consider the similarities and differences between volcanoes and earthquakes.

**VOLCANOES**

- Are formed in different ways
- Produce ash and lava
- Can cause mudslides
- Can bury whole cities
- Can cause great weather changes for long periods of time
- Can create islands and new land forms

**BOTH**

- Occur because of plate movement
- Can cause great destruction
- Occur in the same areas of the earth

**EARTHQUAKES**

- Caused by stress on the earth's crust
- Can cause great drops in land surfaces and deep crevasses
- Can cause large structures to sway and topple
- Occur almost every thirty seconds but most go unnoticed because they are mild shocks

**8.** Use a Venn diagram to present facts about two things. You can choose any topic. Suggestions: compare two of your friends, compare two different places to eat, or compare two cities.

# Outline

When you are not sure how to organize your writing you can create an outline. An outline is a list of the main points you want to cover in your writing, as well as the details you will use to back up your main points.

It is helpful to write your outline in sequential order. All writing has three basic parts: an introduction, a body, and a conclusion.

**Introduction**
- states the topic and main idea of the writing
- includes the Who, What, When, Where, How details

**Body**
- develops the main idea
- tells why things are important or why you feel the way you do
- includes the details to support your main idea

**Conclusion**
- states the results you want to achieve, how you feel about the issue, what you hope the reader has learned

The following is an outline that a student created for a book report.

## Book Report on *Robin Hood*

1. Introduction
   a. title
   b. history of legend
   c. why I chose this book
   d. why I liked it
2. Background of story
   a. the plot
   b. the characters
3. Theme of how the poor should be treated fairly
   a. state theme
   b. give at least three examples of how theme is shown in book
4. My opinion of book
   a. what I liked and why
   b. what I didn't like and why
5. Conclusion
   a. summary of book
   b. summary of my opinion
   c. whether or not I recommend book

Each numbered item in the outline is a major point. The lettered items are the details that explain each major point. When creating an outline of your own, include as much information as possible. Remember, you do not have to include all the outlined ideas in your actual writing.

**9.** Create an outline for a book you have read or a report you need to do for school.

## Tree Diagram

A tree diagram is used to organize a large amount of data. It allows you to create layers of connected information branching out from a central topic. The tree grows from the top down, as you continue to add information to the different branches. A tree diagram is often used to show the genealogy of a family; in that case, it is referred to as a family tree.

The following diagram is an example of a family tree. It lists the people who belong to the Smith-Reilly family. The family members form the branches of the tree.

### Family Tree

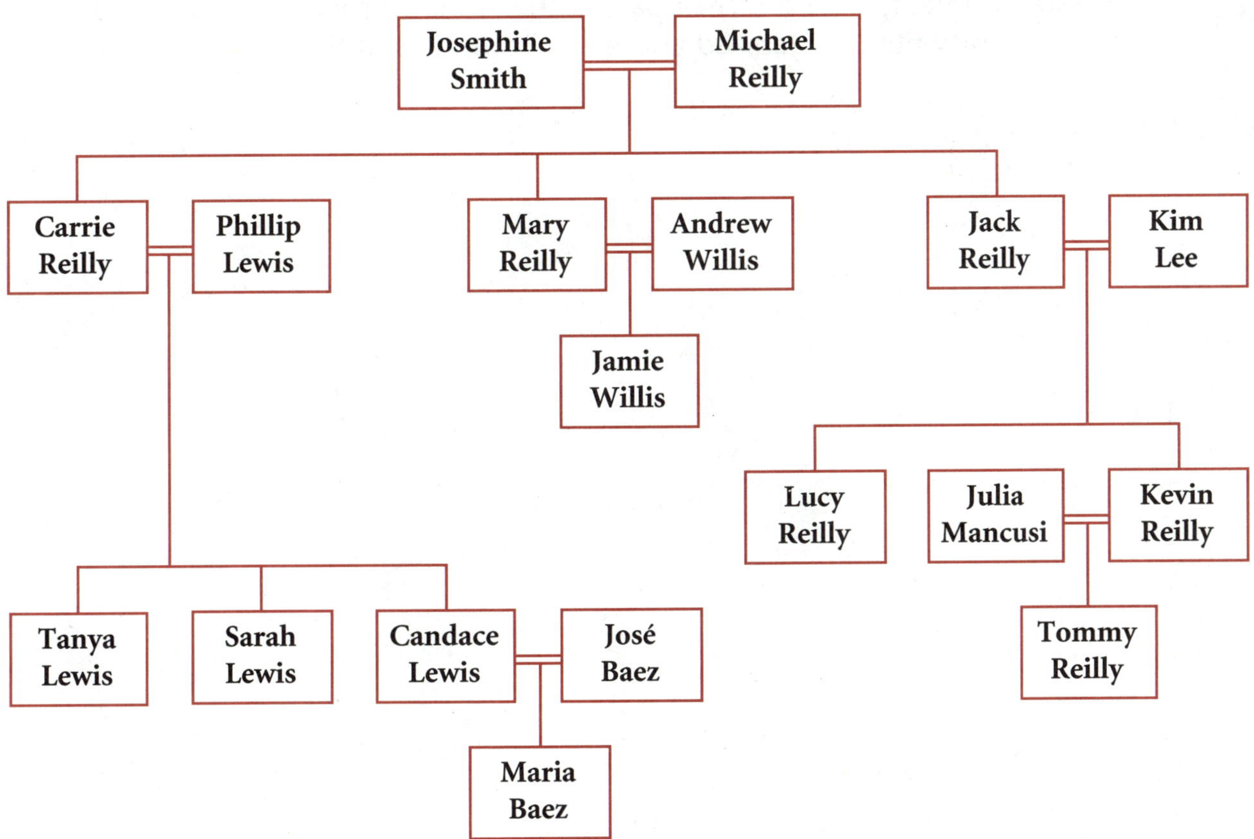

**10.** Pick a topic and create a tree diagram. Possible topics are music, plants, or sports.

## Summary

In this chapter, we have shown you different ways to organize your writing. These strategies will help you get your ideas on paper and organize your thoughts before you begin. Some of these strategies work best with one type of writing. Others can be used with several forms of writing. They are all ways to help you get ready to write.

There are three things to remember. First, you do not need to memorize or follow any of these models exactly. They are suggestions on how to organize your ideas or information. Second, your prewriting model will not be a neat product. You will still need to add, change, delete, and reorganize your ideas after you put them down on paper. That is a major part of prewriting. You work out your problems before you start writing. Finally, do not think of prewriting as a waste of time. It is an essential part of the writing process. It is a way of making your writing organized and easier to understand.

# Unit 2 Writing

## CHAPTER Three

### Get Going

In the previous unit, you read about the importance of prewriting. Now it's time for you to try your hand at writing!

Before writing, think about your topic. Think about what form your writing will take and who your audience will be. You should use a prewriting organizer to help you set up your writing. Once you have your ideas down, you can begin. Remember, you will be writing a first draft. This is your first try. Your writing will not be perfect. There will be changes and corrections that you have to make before you can share your writing with your audience.

### Narrative Text

Narrative text tells a story. The types and forms of the stories will vary. Stories can retell actual events, or they can be completely fictional, or imaginary. Here is your chance to write several different types of stories.

### YOUR Turn

1. Imagine that you are living during another time. It can be in the past or in the future. Write a story about what your life is like.
2. Write a mystery or a science fiction story. Include yourself among the characters.
3. Write a story about a real event that you or someone you know experienced.

## Informational Text

Informational text gives you information on a specific topic. An example of informational text would be a social studies report that you write for school. You may need to do research on a topic to do this type of writing. Sometimes you are asked to respond to something that you have read or studied.

**4.** Think about something related to our environment: air pollution, toxic waste, asbestos, oil spills, or something else. Write a report on the problem, including what you think might correct the situation.

**5.** Write a review of a movie or book that you enjoyed. In your review, tell what you liked the most and why you think others might like the movie or book.

**6.** Pick any subject that you are interested in. It can be something that you know a lot about, or it can be something that you want to know about. Write a report and include as much information as you can.

# Persuasive/Argumentative Text

Persuasive/argumentative text uses argument, reason, facts, and opinion to try to convince you to do something or to think a certain way. The point of persuasive writing is usually to bring about some type of change. To do this, the writer expresses his or her point of view and then tries to persuade the reader that this point of view is correct.

In addition to facts and logic, emotions play a part, too. Many people earn their living persuading us to do, buy, or support something. People running for office try to persuade us to vote for them. Advertising firms work for companies trying to persuade us to buy or use their products. We might be persuaded to buy a product if it is endorsed by a celebrity or if we believe it will improve us or make us more important.

**7.** Pretend you are running for an elected school office. Write a speech that tells your schoolmates what you stand for and why they should vote for you.

**8.** Many people enjoy riding bicycles. However, because there is a lot of traffic on many roads, riding a bike can be dangerous. Write a letter to a government official suggesting that bicycle paths be created in high-traffic areas so that people can ride safely.

**9.** Pretend that you bought something you saw advertised. The product does not live up to the claims made in the advertisement. Write a letter of complaint to either the company, the source of the advertisement, or the Better Business Bureau. Also, make a suggestion as to how the situation could be improved.

## Everyday Text

Everyday text refers to things that we read every day. Its purpose is to give people useful information.

**10.** Write a set of directions to explain how to make or do something. Remember to list the steps in the order in which they should be done.

**11.** A student from another country will be starting school next week. You have been asked to show the student around the school. Write a list of things that you think would be helpful for the new student to know.

# Unit 3 Revising and Editing Strategies

## CHAPTER Four

### Revising Text

The pieces you wrote in Chapter Three are not finished. They are first drafts. First drafts are not perfect. There is always room for improvement. After you finish writing a first draft, you need to read it over carefully. You must ask yourself how it can be improved and where the errors are that need to be corrected. This is called revising and editing.

- Improving what you have written is known as revising.
- Correcting errors, such as spelling, punctuation, and grammar, is known as editing.

All writers go through these two steps to improve their writing. The better the writing, the more understandable it is to your audience.

There are many ways to revise a first draft. Sometimes writers do a complete rewrite. However, most times you revise your writing by doing the following:

- adding information
- deleting (removing) information
- rearranging (moving) information
- combining sentences
- adding transitional, or signal, words and phrases

Keep in mind that often there is no right or wrong when revising a draft. Every writer has a style. You will revise your writing according to your own personal style. Do not be afraid to try different ways of revising your work.

## Adding Information

When you reread your first draft, you may decide that you left out something important. You will find that you need to add something to make your writing clearer. Do not be afraid to make these changes.

Here is an example of when adding information improves the text:

**Draft**

Hong spoke with his music teacher about what type of musical piece he should play. The teacher thinks that Hong should play a classical composition.

The draft leaves many unanswered questions, such as "Why did Hong speak with the music teacher?" and "Why does the music teacher suggest he play a classical composition?"

Hong is competing for a music award at the spring concert. He

~~Hong~~ spoke with his music teacher about what type of musical piece he should play. The teacher thinks that Hong should play a classical ~~composition.~~

piece because he is gifted and would best display his talent with a classical composition.

**Revision**

Hong is competing for a music award at the spring concert. He spoke with his music teacher about which musical piece he should play. The teacher thinks that Hong should play a classical piece because he is gifted and would best display his talent with a classical composition.

Here is another example:

**Draft**

Tori is concerned about Max. He wandered off early this morning and has not returned home. She thinks she should call him.

The most important information left out of this draft is that Max is a cat. Adding that to the first sentence greatly improves the draft. The writer also decided to add an extra sentence to clear up why Tori thinks she should call Max.

**Revision**

Tori is concerned about her cat Max. He wandered off early this morning and has not returned home. She thinks she should call him. When Max hears Tori call his name, he usually comes home.

The added information explains who Max is and tells the reader more about the situation.

**1.** Revise the draft on museums by adding information.

Museums offer us a window on the past, the future, and the greatness of the human spirit. There are many different kinds of museums.

Decide what is missing. Think about what information could be added to help explain what the paragraph is about. For example, you might want to give a few different examples of museums and what they exhibit.

**2.** Add information to this paragraph.

Most every nation has a song of its own, just as it has a flag of its own. This song has been named by the government to be the "national anthem."

## Deleting Information

Sometimes information or sentences need to be deleted from your writing. You might need to keep your writing brief. Or, after reading your draft, you realize that you have included unnecessary information.

Here is an example of when deleting information improves the text:

***Draft***

People have been building tunnels since around 2000 B.C. At that time, the ancient Persians dug them to move water from one place to another. Later, in India and Egypt, people often buried their dead in tunnels. In the fifteenth century, warring armies learned to dig tunnels under their enemies. They would then travel through these holes in order to stage surprise attacks. These sudden attacks were planned to catch the enemy off guard. Today, some tunnels let us travel through mountains and under rivers. Others allow water to be brought to big cities. And still others are built under large cities to house water pipes as well as lines for electric, telephone, and gas services. I like the idea of these lines being under the ground so that we don't have to look at them.

The sixth sentence repeats information stated in the fifth sentence. Since the sixth sentence gives no new information, it should be deleted. Also, the last sentence is the writer's opinion and does not belong in this type of informational paragraph.

People have been building tunnels since around 2000 B.C. At that time, the ancient Persians dug them to move water from one place to another. Later, in India and Egypt, people often buried their dead in tunnels. In the fifteenth century, warring armies learned to dig tunnels under their enemies. They would then travel through these holes in order to stage surprise attacks. ~~These sudden attacks were planned to catch the enemy off guard.~~ Today, some tunnels let us travel through mountains and under rivers. Others allow water to be brought to big cities. And still others are built under large cities to house water pipes as well as lines for electric, telephone, and gas services. ~~I like the idea of these lines being under the ground so that we don't have to look at them.~~

**Revision**

People have been building tunnels since around 2000 B.C. At that time, the ancient Persians dug them to move water from one place to another. Later, in India and Egypt, people often buried their dead in tunnels. In the fifteenth century, warring armies learned to dig tunnels under their enemies. They would then travel through these holes in order to stage surprise attacks. Today, some tunnels let us travel through mountains and under rivers. Others allow water to be brought to big cities. And still others are built under large cities to house water pipes as well as lines for electric, telephone, and gas services.

Sometimes you need to delete only a few extra words in your writing to make it read more smoothly. You might be able to get rid of the word altogether or replace it.

**Draft**

Guinea pigs were brought to Europe by the Dutch in the 1500s. But guinea pigs originally came from South America, particularly from Guyana. In fact, the name "guinea pig" comes from "Guiana pig." The "pig" part refers to the guinea pig's piglike appearance. However, guinea pigs are not pigs. Guinea pigs are rodents. Guinea pigs have four toes on their front feet and three toes on their hind feet. Guinea pigs have small round ears, weigh about one pound, grow up to fourteen inches long, and have no tails. Timid animals, guinea pigs frighten easily and utter loud whistlelike screams when threatened.

The term *guinea pigs* is used too many times in this draft. When some of them are taken out or replaced, the paragraph will read better.

**Revision**

Guinea pigs were brought to Europe by the Dutch in the 1500s. But they originally came from South America, particularly from Guyana. In fact, their name comes from "Guiana pig." The "pig" part refers to the animal's piglike appearance. However, guinea pigs are not pigs, but rodents. They have four toes on their front feet and three toes on their hind feet. They have small round ears, weigh about one pound, grow up to fourteen inches long, and have no tails. Timid animals, these rodents frighten easily and utter loud whistlelike screams when threatened.

**3.** Revise the draft below by deleting information.

Scientists believe there is no life on Jupiter. One reason is the temperature—about 170° below zero. That is too cold for any form of life as we know it to exist. Animals and plants could not survive in such a cold temperature. Another reason scientists think that there is no life on Jupiter is the atmosphere. Jupiter's air has no oxygen, but it does contain a deadly gas called methane. Even if humans visit Jupiter wearing protective spacesuits and carrying oxygen, they would find it impossible to walk. The gravity is over two and a half times greater than on Earth. I would hate to live on Jupiter because I would weigh much more.

Which sentences or parts of sentences could be deleted without harming the text?

**4.** Delete the unnecessary information in the following paragraph:

Vikings believed that dead warriors went to a spirit world called Valhalla. There are many other cultures that also believe in a spirit world. Ships often played an important part in the funerals of wealthy Vikings. The Viking ships were packed with weapons, dishes, and food for use in the spirit world. They thought these goods could be used in the new life in Valhalla. Ships were either buried or burned. Some Vikings burned the funeral ships because they believed the smoke would help the warrior's spirit rise to Valhalla. In 1904, scientists in Norway found two women buried in a beautiful ship filled with carvings and ornaments.

# Rearranging Information

Sometimes your writing will read better if some sentences or paragraphs are moved to different places in the text. This is known as rearranging, or reordering, information. This revision strategy is especially useful when you are writing something in a sequential or chronological order.

Here is a paragraph that needs some rearranging.

***Draft***

Put the bandage on firmly enough to do the job, but not so tight as to stop the flow of blood. A bandage should not be applied directly to an open wound; the wound should first be covered with a sterile gauze compress. When bandaging has been completed, check to make sure that it is not too tight, because injury often causes swelling. After the bandage is applied, fasten it with adhesive tape. If the patient complains of the bandage being too tight or painful, reapply the bandage. It is better to do this than to take a chance on stopping the blood supply to the injured part. Another way to fasten the bandage is to split the free end of the bandage to form two tails, bring one around the bandaged part, and tie the two ends with a square knot.

The events in this paragraph are out of sequence. Rearrange the steps so that they are in the correct order.

Put the bandage on firmly enough to do the job, but not so tight as to stop the flow of blood. A bandage should not be applied directly to an open wound; the wound should first be covered with a sterile gauze compress. When bandaging has been completed, check to make sure that it is not too tight, because injury often causes swelling. After the bandage is applied, fasten it with adhesive tape. If the patient complains of the bandage being too tight or painful, reapply the bandage. It is better to do this than to take a chance on stopping the blood supply to the injured part. Another way to fasten the bandage is to split the free end of the bandage to form two tails, bring one around the bandaged part, and tie the two ends with a square knot.

**Revision**

A bandage should not be applied directly to an open wound; the wound should first be covered with a sterile gauze compress. Put the bandage on firmly enough to do the job, but not so tight as to stop the flow of blood. After the bandage is applied, fasten it with adhesive tape. Another way to fasten the bandage is to split the free end of the bandage to form two tails, bring one around the bandaged part, and tie the two ends with a square knot. When bandaging has been completed, check to make sure that it is not too tight, because injury often causes swelling. If the patient complains of the bandage being too tight or painful, reapply the bandage. It is better to do this than to take a chance on stopping the blood supply to the injured part.

Here is another paragraph that will read better after some rearranging.

**Draft**

Repeat the steps until he eagerly goes into the begging position to earn dog candy. Here's how to teach your dog to beg. First, place the dog in the sitting position with the proper command. Hold him that way until he finds a comfortable balance, and then let him balance himself. Then, lift his front paws up until he is in a begging position. As he gets his balance, hold a dog treat over his nose. As soon as you let go of his front paws, lower the treat to his mouth and let him take it from your hands. Hold the dog treat firmly so it takes a few seconds for him to pry it loose; during this time, say "BEG" over and over. From then on, you must bribe him with a treat until he assumes the begging position upon the command BEG.

The first sentence belongs at the end of the paragraph. And the fourth sentence should follow the sentence beginning with the words "Then, lift his front paws."

**Revision**

Here's how to teach your dog to beg. First, place the dog in the sitting position with the proper command. Then, lift his front paws up until he is in a begging position. Hold him that way until he finds a comfortable balance, and then let him balance himself. As he gets his balance, hold a dog treat over his nose. As soon as you let go of his front paws, lower the treat to his mouth and let him take it from your hands. Hold the dog treat firmly so it takes a few seconds for him to pry it loose; during this time, say "BEG" over and over. From then on, you must bribe him with a treat until he assumes the begging position upon the command BEG. Repeat the steps until he eagerly goes into the begging position to earn dog candy.

**5.** The following excerpt adapted from *The Adventures of Tom Sawyer* by Mark Twain has been scrambled. Rearrange the sentences in the paragraph into their logical order.

He surveyed the fence, and all gladness left him and a deep sadness settled upon his spirit. There were thirty yards of board fence, nine feet high. Tom appeared on the sidewalk with a bucket of whitewash and a long-handled brush. Life to him seemed hollow, and existence but a burden. He repeated the operation, and did it again. He compared the small whitewashed streak with the far-reaching stretch of unwhitewashed fence. Sighing, he dipped his brush and passed it along the topmost plank. He sat down on a tree-box, discouraged.

After rearranging the sentences, read the paragraph to see if it makes sense.

**6.** The following sentences have been scrambled. Rearrange the sentences in the paragraph into their logical order.

Clara Barton was born December 25, 1821, in a farm near Oxford, Massachusetts. During the Civil War she volunteered to carry supplies to soldiers and to nurse men wounded on the battlefields. She became a teacher at the age of fifteen. At thirty-three she took a position as a government clerk in Washington, D.C., where she remained until the Civil War. When the Civil War ended, she formed and headed a group to search for missing soldiers. Barton went to Switzerland in 1869. In 1871, during the Franco-Prussian War, she served as a nurse at the battlefront. After eight years, the United States became a member of the International Red Cross, and Clara Barton became the first president of the American Red Cross. She returned home in 1873, and encouraged the United States to join the Red Cross, an organization newly founded in Switzerland.

# Combining Sentences

There are times when your writing can be improved simply by combining two or more ideas or sentences into a single sentence.

Here is an example of a revision made by combining sentences.

**Draft**

Pablo got a part-time job. He saved his money. So he was able to buy a new CD player.

There are a number of ways that these sentences can be combined. Here is one possible way of combining them.

Because

Pablo got a part-time job. He saved his money. So he was able to buy a new CD player.

and ,

**Revision**

Because Pablo got a part-time job and saved his money, he was able to buy a new CD player.

Here is another piece of writing that is improved by combining sentences.

**Draft**

Marcia is in the bookstore. She is looking for a book about computers. At the same time, her mother is returning a sweater in the department store.

Here is one possible way of combining these ideas.

**Revision**

While Marcia is in the bookstore looking for a book about computers, her mother is returning a sweater in the department store.

**7.** Revise this paragraph by combining sentences.

The barracuda is a saltwater fish. The barracuda looks very much like the pike. The pike is a freshwater fish. The barracuda is not related to the pike. It is like that freshwater fish in being a fearless fighter. The barracuda has a large mouth. It also has strong jaws that hold knifelike teeth. When attacking or defending itself, the barracuda moves like lightning. It usually feeds on other fish. It has been known to attack swimmers.

Look for the short sentences. Those are the ones that can most easily be combined. Also, combining sentences eliminates unnecessary repetitions of certain words.

**8.** Combine the following thirteen sentences into eight or less sentences.

The Sahara Desert is the world's largest desert. It stretches 3,200 miles across northern Africa. It covers 3.5 million square miles. This desert is almost as large as the United States. It is home to more than three million people. Dunes in the Sahara may be many miles long and pile over 500 feet high. The largest is the Great Sand Sea. It covers an area the size of France. Sand covers only one-fifth of the entire area of the Sahara. Much of the rest of the Sahara is covered by stones and rock. There are also lakes. One of these is Lake Chad. It is the size of the state of New Jersey.

## Adding Transitional, or Signal, Words and Phrases

Transitional, or signal, words are important in writing. They create a smooth transition from one paragraph or idea to another. They help the reader follow your thoughts. Transitional words give important clues as to the sequence in which things happen. They can also signal a change in the writer's thinking, as well as serve other purposes.

Some transitional words are as follows:

| | | |
|---|---|---|
| after | first | next |
| also | however | so |
| as a result | in addition | suddenly |
| at last | later | then |
| because | likewise | therefore |
| but | meanwhile | when |
| finally | moreover | yet |

You can use transitional words or phrases

- to combine two sentences.
- to help the reader see relationships between paragraphs.
- to help the reader know what is coming next.

Here is an example of when writing can be revised using a transitional word.

**Draft**

Barry forgot to study for the test. He did not receive a good grade. He made up his mind to be better prepared for the next text.

These sentences read better when the transitional words *because* and *as a result* are added.



**Revision**

Because Barry forgot to study for the test, he did not receive a good grade. As a result, he made up his mind to be better prepared for the next test.

Here is a revision made by adding a transitional phrase between paragraphs.

**Draft**

Nida got a job after school taking care of some neighbors' pets. She would walk and exercise the dogs, and give them a bath every other week. She didn't make much money, but she enjoyed working with animals.

Nida found a job working in an animal shelter. Now Nida's sister looks after the neighbors' dogs and Nida can do the work she enjoys and make good money, too.

A transitional word would better connect these two paragraphs. The last sentence of the first paragraph lets the reader know that Nida is not totally happy with her job and sets the stage for what is to come. The transitional phrase *after several months* ties the two paragraphs together.

**Revision**

Nida got a job after school taking care of some neighbors' pets. She would walk and exercise the dogs, and give them a bath every other week. She didn't make much money, but she enjoyed working with animals.

After several months, Nida found a job working in an animal shelter. Now Nida's sister looks after the neighbors' dogs and Nida can do the work she enjoys and make good money, too.

**9.** Combine these sentences using a transitional word or phrase.

> Cara was a very good speaker. She decided to try out for the debating team.

There is more than one transitional word or phrase that could be used here. Choose whichever one you feel sounds the best in the writing.

**10.** Which transitional word or phrase would improve the flow of the text between the paragraphs?

> When the United States Civil War broke out, many free blacks in the North volunteered to join the army. All were turned down. "This is a white man's war," they were told.
>
> In the fall of 1862, blacks were taken into the army. They received lower pay than white soldiers and were kept in segregated units with white officers, but they fought boldly and skillfully. By the end of the war, 38,000 black soldiers and sailors had died for the promise of freedom for all African Americans.

## SUMMARY

You have had the opportunity to learn and practice five important strategies necessary for revising your writing. They are as follows:

- adding information
- deleting information
- rearranging information
- combining sentences
- adding transitional, or signal, words and phrases

All of these strategies are part of the writing process. All writers use one, or perhaps all, of them to perfect their drafts. You should do the same.

In the next chapter, we will discuss the editing process. This is another step you need to take in order to polish your writing before it is read by others.

# CHAPTER Five

## Editing Text

Now that you have learned different ways of revising a text, the next step is to learn to edit your writing. When you edit, you check that you have spelled words correctly, used the correct punctuation, capitalized words where needed, and followed the rules of good grammar and sentence structure. Before you share your writing with readers, you want to check it carefully for errors. When you have done this, you are ready to prepare your final draft.

When editing, apply what you already know about the rules of grammar. In this chapter, we will look at three areas of difficulty:

- spelling
- capitalization
- punctuation

When you edit your writing, it is a good idea to check for only one type of error at a time. This will help you find more errors because you can think about one skill at a time.

## Spelling

No one is expected to know how to spell every word. You should use a dictionary, a spell-check program on your computer, or have someone else proofread your work.

It is important to check your spelling to avoid mistakes. However, do not let concerns about spelling get in the way of your writing. If you do, you will never increase your vocabulary. If you use the same words over and over again, your reader will lose interest in what you are saying.

There are many ways that you can improve your spelling:

- Often you can tell a word is not spelled correctly just by looking at it. Sometimes you will find errors by saying the word aloud or writing the word as you spell it. Once you have the correct spelling, write the word several times.
- Many English textbooks contain a list of words that are easy to misspell. Study these words so that you learn to spell them correctly.
- Write down words that *you* often misspell in a notebook. Use tabs with letters on them to help put the words in alphabetical order. This will make it easier to look them up later.
- A similar method is to put words on index cards. The cards can be kept in a card file box, organized with a set of alphabetical tabs to make the words easier to find.
- Read your written material backward, from the end to the beginning, and from the bottom to the top of the page. This allows you to look at the spelling of the words themselves and not the content.
- Remember that when you use a word-processing program on a computer, the spell check will only tell you if the word is spelled correctly, not if it is the correct word. For instance, with homonyms like *there* and *their*, a spell check will not be able to tell you when you have used the incorrect form of a word.

# YOUR Turn

**1.** Here is a brief passage. Read it and underline all the spelling errors you find.

The sky was high and brite. I lay back on the gras in the infeild of the track and laziley watched the thin white clowds evaperate in the warm morning air. It was pieceful. In a groove of trees on the other side of the track, a bird sprang into song. Litely, I dozed. With the earth at my back and the sun above me, I felt surounded by great forses of growth and heet. Enirgy flowed into my body. I felt strong.

It was Saturday. In one weak, I would step out onto a track in another countrey. I would stand sholder to sholder with five other yong men at the starting line of the 200-meter race. We wood be called to our marks. We would crowch at the line, our feat in the starting blocks. Would I have what it would take to win?

Sudenly, I was brougt back to the presint by someone shouting my name. "Hey, Richard," the coach called, "are you going to trane today? You must be extremly confidant. Come on, get up. We have work to do."

**2.** Rewrite the passage, correcting all of the spelling errors.

## Capitalization

After you have corrected the spelling errors in your draft, your next step is to check for errors in capitalization.

Capitalize the following:

- **Proper nouns**—*a particular person, place, or thing*
  Warren Jones, Jasper National Park, Eiffel Tower
- **Proper adjectives**—*formed from a proper noun*
  Canadian, Californian
- **Historical events**—*names of events, documents, and periods of time*
  World War II, Magna Carta, Middle Ages
- **Names of peoples, races, tribes, and languages**—
  Rock Dwellers, Caucasian, Pygmy, French
- **Geographical names**—*planets and heavenly bodies, continents, countries, states, provinces, counties, cities, bodies of water, landforms, public areas, roads and highways, and buildings*
  North Pole, Mars, Mexico, Atlantic Ocean, Eternal City
- **Organizations**—
  International Red Cross, Boy Scouts
- **First word in a sentence and a direct quotation**—
  Hamlet said, "To be, or not to be."
- **Particular section of a country**—
  Midwest, West Coast
- **Religions and religious terms**—
  Protestant, Islam, Advent, Jehovah, Old Testament
- **Names and words used as names**—
  Grandma Moses, Dad, Aunt Sarah, Dr. Perez
- **Days of the week, months, holidays**—
  Monday, June, Christmas
- **Official names of businesses, products, and trademarks**—
  Rolls Royce, Coca Cola, Kodak
- **Titles that precede names**—
  Prime Minister Denner, Bishop Perkins, General Manager Dillon

- **First, last, and all important words (nouns, pronouns, verbs, adjectives, adverbs) in titles of books, songs, movies, etc.—** *Moby Dick, The New York Times,* "Mona Lisa"

When you are using titles of individuals, capitalize the title only if the person's name follows (Vice President Bailey). If the name is not used, do not capitalize the title (We spoke to the vice president).

**3.** This passage has no capitalization in it. Find all the words that need to be capitalized and circle them.

maffeo and niccolo polo were two merchants in venice, italy, in the late 1200s. they heard of the riches of far-off cathay, now known as china, and they decided to journey there. in 1271, they set off from venice with niccolo's seventeen-year-old son, marco.

the polos crossed the mediterranean sea and then traveled by land—sometimes on horses, sometimes on camels, and sometimes on foot. they saw things more wonderful than anything known in europe at that time. after three years, they reached the court of emperor kublai khan.

the polos lived at the court of kublai khan for 17 years. the emperor took a special interest in marco and made him an official of the court. far and wide marco traveled in the lands of the khan. nothing escaped his keen eyes. years later when marco was aprisoner in the city of genoa, he told the story of his travels to another prisoner who knew how to write. as a result, people everywhere learned about the wonders of the east.

# Punctuation

## Period, Question Mark, Exclamation Point

All sentences end with a *period*, a *question mark*, or an *exclamation point*. A common mistake is using a period after a group of words that is not a complete sentence. These are sentence fragments, and they lack a subject (who or what the sentence is about) or a predicate (the verb).

## Comma

The most often used punctuation mark is the *comma*. A comma should be used only to make the meaning of a sentence clearer. It is used to separate words, such as the city and state in an address (Newark, New Jersey) or a series of items in a sentence (Bring your book, ruler, and pencil).

There are three main uses of a comma. You use a comma to separate two independent clauses joined by a coordinating conjunction, to separate who is speaking from a direct quotation, and to separate the introductory word or group of words at the beginning of a sentence from the rest of the sentence.

Let's look at a few examples of these three uses.

- To separate two independent clauses joined by a coordinating conjunction

> The teacher lectured for thirty minutes, and then he gave the students a surprise quiz.

Two independent clauses can be written as two sentences. For example, the teacher lectured for thirty minutes. Then he gave the students a surprise quiz. When you join the two, you need a comma after the first clause, before the coordinating conjunction. Common coordinating conjunctions are *and*, *or*, and *but*.

> Jeff was good enough to make the baseball team, but he preferred to play soccer.

- To separate who is speaking from a direct quotation

> Tina answered, "I'll meet you at the movie theater after dinner."

The words *Tina answered* are not part of the quote. They are outside of the quotation marks and must be separated from the quote by a comma.

> "Don't worry, I won't be late," she insisted.

- To separate the word or words introducing a sentence from the rest of the sentence

> Meanwhile, the children waited restlessly for the movie to begin.

The subject of the sentence is *the children,* not *meanwhile. Meanwhile* is just an introductory word that should be set off by a comma.

In the following example, a comma is used after an introductory phrase.

> After the movie was over, the children begged to see it again.

## Semicolons and Colons

The *semicolon* is another way to separate ideas in a sentence. When you have two independent clauses and do not use a coordinating conjunction, you need a semicolon. Let's look at another example.

The doctor examined me, and then she prescribed some medicine for my cough.

To join these two clauses without the word *and*, you need to use the semicolon.

The doctor examined me; then she prescribed some medicine for my cough.

Another use of the semicolon is to separate groups of words that contain commas within them.

Invitations to the conference have been sent to sales managers in Little Rock, Arkansas; Sante Fe, New Mexico; Albany, New York; and Lincoln, Nebraska.

Without the semicolons, this sentence would be difficult to read due to all the commas.

You use a *colon* before a list or to introduce something that follows, such as a direct question or quotation, an example, or to expand upon what has come before. A colon cannot follow a verb or preposition. Look at the examples shown here.

The attractive features of the house are as follows: two bathrooms, a finished basement, and a fireplace.

While in London, England, be sure to see these sights: Westminster Abbey, the Tower of London, Buckingham Palace, and Piccadilly Circus.

The math test on Friday will cover the following: fractions, decimals, and percentages.

# Apostrophe

The *apostrophe* is another punctuation mark. While it has several uses, the two most common are to show possession (Mary's book) and to indicate a contraction (don't). A common error people make is confusing plurals that end in the letter *s* (girls), possessives (girl's), and the possessive of a word ending in *s* (girls').

Here are some examples that may help clarify the situation.

The above sentence refers to more than one girl. *Girls* is a plural noun, not a word showing ownership.

The girl's goal won the game.

The word *girl* needs an apostrophe before the letter *s* to show possession, or that it is her goal.

The girls' team is now in first place.

This sentence indicates that we are referring to more than one girl, and their team is in first place. Begin with the plural word *girls*, and then add an apostrophe after the letter *s* to show possession.

## Quotation Marks

*Quotation marks* are another form of punctuation that can cause problems. When a direct quotation ends with a comma or a period, the final set of quotation marks are always placed after the comma or period.

"I must return these boots to the shoe store," Midori explained. Elsa replied, "I'll go with you. I want to see if there are any shoes on sale."

Exclamation points and question marks are placed inside the quotation marks when they punctuate the quotation. But when they punctuate the main sentence, they are placed outside the quotation marks.

Kevin asked, "May I use your computer this weekend?"

Did Owen mean it when he said, "I'm not going to the dance"?

Most of the time, however, the final punctuation for a direct quotation will be inside the set of quotation marks. Ask yourself, does the punctuation refer to the sentence itself or to the quote?

4. This passage needs two types of punctuation: periods and question marks. Mark the changes right on the passage.

Have you ever heard of Jean Lafitte He was a pirate who became a patriot Arriving in New Orleans in 1803, he was readily accepted and admired by the French citizens there Why did they admire a pirate Lafitte was no ordinary pirate He was a gallant and handsome gentleman who spoke several languages He was a respected businessman and a welcome guest in the best homes of the city

Lafitte was a French privateer sailing under the flag of the Republic of Cartagena Because of his commission as a privateer, he claimed that his seizure of Spanish ships sailing the Caribbean was legal How did the new American government in New Orleans view Lafitte To the American government, Lafitte's activities violated many trade laws and he was thus considered a criminal Spurred on by angry shipowners whom Lafitte had robbed, Governor Claiborne charged him with piracy and smuggling

Then, in 1812, America went to war with England Lafitte commanded more than 1000 men and a fleet of ships The English offered him a large sum of money if he would aid them in attacking New Orleans What do you think Lafitte did You might be surprised to learn that he informed his old enemy, Governor Claiborne, of the British plans He then offered his fleet and the services of his men to the United States government Could the governor trust this pirate He decided to take a chance on Lafitte's sincerity And it was a good thing that he did Without Lafitte and his men, the Battle of New Orleans might have been lost to the British

**5.** Read the story carefully. Write in commas and apostrophes where they are needed.

A hungry wolf chanced one night to meet with a plump house dog. After the first greetings were exchanged the wolf said "How is it that you look so plump? And here am I barely able to save myself from starving."

"Well" said the dog "if you want to be well fed as I am you have to do as I do."

"And whats that?" asked the wolf.

"Just guard the masters house and keep thieves away."

"Gladly" said the wolf. "Some might like the forest life but its too hard a life for me."

"Just follow me" replied the dog.

As the two were strolling along together the wolf noticed a mark on the dogs neck. Being curious he could not resist asking what it meant.

"Oh nothing at all" replied the dog. "Perhaps the collar to which my chain is fastened was too tight."

"You dont mean that youre not free to roam about as you please?" asked the wolf.

"Well not exactly" explained the dog. "You see Im considered very fierce so sometimes they tie me up in the daytime. But at night Im free and my master feeds me off his own plate. Whats the matter? Where are you going?"

"Good-bye" said the wolf. "Youre welcome to all of the luxuries. As for me a dry crust of bread with my liberty is more important than a kings luxury with a chain."

**6.** This passage needs colons and semicolons. Read the passage and put the punctuation where it belongs.

Many people enjoy playing board games such as the following backgammon, checkers, and chess. Chess is a game for two played upon a checkered board with movable pieces called men it is played in nearly every civilized country. Nobody is sure where the game of chess was first played. It may have spread from country to country in the following order India, Persia, and Spain.

Each chess player has the following men one king, one queen, two bishops, two knights, two rooks, and eight pawns. Each type of piece has powers particular to itself the queen is the most powerful piece on the board. The object of the game is to capture the opponent's king various advantages such as the capture of enemy men may have to be gained before that objective can be accomplished. A good chess player must have the following qualities a quick mind, a good memory, and foresight.

In addition to the type of chess most people play, some other types of chess are as follows computer chess, postal chess, blindfold chess, and lightning chess. Some board games that resemble chess are checkers, a game played on the same board as chess go, a Japanese game and Chinese checkers.

**7.** This following passage, adapted from *A Christmas Carol* by Charles Dickens, needs quotation marks. Read the passage and mark where the punctuation needs to go.

Merry Christmas, Uncle! cried a cheerful voice. It was the voice of Scrooge's nephew, who came upon him so quickly that this was the first knowledge he had of his approach.

Bah! said Scrooge. Humbug!

This nephew of Scrooge's had so heated himself with rapid walking in the fog and frost that he was all in a glow. His eyes sparkled, and his breath smoked.

Christmas a humbug, Uncle! said Scrooge's nephew. You don't mean that, I'm sure.

I do, said Scrooge. Merry Christmas! What right have you to be merry? You're poor enough.

Come then, returned the nephew, gaily. What right have you to be dismal? You're rich enough.

Scrooge, having no better answer ready on the spur of the moment, said, Bah! again, and followed it up with Humbug.

Don't be cross, Uncle, said the nephew.

What else can I be, returned the uncle, when I live in such a world of fools as this? Merry Christmas! What's Christmastime to you but a time for paying bills without money. If I could work my will, every idiot who goes about with 'Merry Christmas' on his lips should be boiled in his own pudding and buried with a stake of holly through his heart. He should!

Uncle! pleaded the nephew.

Nephew! returned the uncle, sternly. Keep Christmas in your own way, and let me keep it in mine.

# Unit 4 Practice Revising and Editing

## CHAPTER Six

## Modeled Instruction

Many tests include exercises that test your revising and editing skills. Usually, you are given a writing sample filled with errors and asked multiple-choice questions about how the sample should be revised. In this chapter, you will find writing samples of three different types of writing: informational, persuasive/argumentative, and everyday text. After each sample are multiple-choice questions such as the kind you would find on tests. We will show you some strategies that will help you answer these questions.

# Informational Text

The following passage tells about Vietnamese puppet shows. Read the passage and then answer the questions that follow.

## The Vietnamese Puppet Theater

The Vietnamese have a type of puppet theater that is not like any other. As with other puppet theaters, it is performed with marionettes—complete, jointed puppets operated by strings. Instead of using a solid stage, these puppets perform on water! In many Eastern countries, the traditional puppet plays that have been performed for many centuries may still be seen.

For about 1,000 years, troupes of water puppeteers have journeyed across vietnam to perform on its many rivers and lakes. They create their theater by setting up screens of braided reeds on the water. These screens serve to prevent the audience from seeing the puppeteers operate the marionettes. Its a soggy job, for the puppeteers often stand in water up to their waists.

The wooden marionettes are brightly painted in shades of gold and red. Attached to small wooden platforms. They stand from one and a half to two feet high. Each puppet is moved on the surface of the water by means of underwater rods that can be as long as thirty feet. Wires, strings, and other devises are used to make the puppets come alive. The chief character is Teu. He is a smiling marionette who narrates the story.

1. What transition is needed at the beginning of the sentence in lines 4–5 ("Instead...water!")?
   A. First,
   B. In addition,
   C. For example,
   D. However,

Look for the word or phrase that will connect this sentence with the previous one. Try each choice and see which best suits the situation.

2. Which sentence should be omitted because it does NOT support the focus of paragraph 1?
   A. lines 2–3 ("The...other.")
   B. lines 3–4 ("As...strings.")
   C. lines 4–5 ("Instead...water!")
   D. lines 5–7 ("In...seen.")

What is the paragraph about? Which sentence has nothing to do with the focus of the paragraph?

3. What editing change, if any, is needed in lines 8–9 ("For...lakes.")?
   A. Delete the comma after *years*.
   B. Change *troupes* to *troups*.
   C. Change *vietnam* to *Vietnam*.
   D. Make no change.

For choice A, you must remember the rules for adding commas. Does a comma belong after the introductory phrase? For choice B, decide which spelling is correct. And for choice C, you must remember the rules of capitalization. Is there any reason to capitalize this word? If everything is correct as is, then choice D is your answer.

**4.** What editing change, if any, is needed in lines 11–12 ("These...marionettes.")?

A. Place a comma after *audience.*

B. Change *puppeteers* to *puppeteer's*

C. Change the period to an exclamation point.

D. Make no change.

Does a comma belong in the sentence? Does the sentence talk about something that belongs to the puppeteers? Is there enough emotion in the sentence to warrant an exclamation point? If the answer to all these questions is no, then the correct answer is choice D.

**5.** What editing change, if any, is needed in lines 12–13 ("Its...waists.")?

A. Change *Its* to *It's.*

B. Change the comma after *job* to a semicolon.

C. Change *their* to *there.*

D. Make no change.

Choice A asks you to choose between a possessive and a contraction. Which one belongs in the sentence? Choice B asks you to distinguish between using a comma and a semicolon. Do you remember the rules for both? And choice C presents two words that sound alike. Do you need a pronoun in the sentence or an adverb?

**6.** What editing change, if any, is needed in lines 15–16 ("Attached...high.")?

A. Change the period after *platforms* to a colon and change *They* to *they*.

B. Change the period after *platforms* to a comma and change *They* to *they*.

C. Delete the period after *platforms* and change *They* to *they*.

D. Make no change.

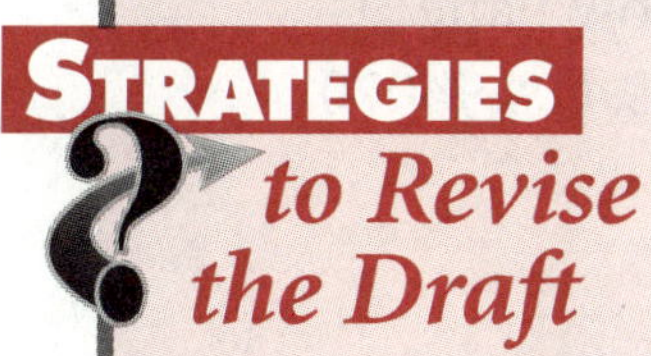


This question requires you to remember the rules of punctuation. Read each choice to see if an editing change will result in a correctly punctuated sentence. If everything is correct as is, no change is needed.

**7.** What editing change, if any, is needed in lines 18–19 ("Wires...alive.")?

A. Delete the comma after *strings*.

B. Change *devises* to *devices*.

C. Change *come* to *came*.

D. Make no change.

For choice A, do you remember the rules for adding commas to a series? For choice B, which word is correct for the sense of the sentence—*devises* or *devices*? And for choice C, is there any reason to change the tense of the verb from the present to the past? Here's a clue: the tense should remain the same throughout the sentence.

**8.** What is the BEST way to combine the sentences in lines 19–20 ("The...story.")?

A. A smiling marionette narrates the story, and his name is Teu.

B. A smiling marionette, the chief character, narrates the story.

C. The chief character is Teu, a smiling marionette who narrates the story.

D. Because Teu is the chief character, he narrates the story as a smiling marionette.

You need to combine the two sentences into one correct sentence. The answer must contain all the important information from both sentences. It must also be worded clearly and logically.

# Persuasive/Argumentative Text

David believes that there should be a traffic light at the corner of Seventh and Main Streets. He wrote a letter to the mayor to express his feelings. Read David's letter and then answer the questions that follow.

150 Meadow Lane
San Carlos, CA 94070

Mayor Loretta Seballos
City Hall
75 Fifth Avenue
San Carlos, CA 94070

Dear mayor Seballos:

I believe that there should be a traffic light at the corner of Sixth and Main Streets. This is a dangerous corner to cross. Although cars are suposed to be traveling no more than 30 miles per hour in the school zone, most go much faster than that. And many kids cross this busy corner as they walk back and forth to school. Another busy corner is the one at the intersection of Maple and Fern Avenues.

The lack of a traffic light has had serious results. Since school began in September, there have been four accidents at that crossing that have injured students. One of these students died as a result of her injuries. There have also been several other near misses, I myself was almost hit by a car while crossing Main Street.

In the winter, it is already dark by the time we get to that crossing after school. There is also a lot of traffic at those hours. The reason for this is that some people are driving home from work. Often you have to try to run across when there is not enough time. The students would be much safer if there were a light.

Yours truly
David Kovac

**9.** What revision, if any, is needed in lines 1–2?

A. Add a period after *Lane*.

B. Add the date.

C. Put the ZIP code on a separate line.

D. Make no change.

Think about the opening of a letter. Decide what punctuation is needed. Should any other information be added?

**10.** What editing change, if any, is needed in line 7?

A. Change *mayor* to *Mayor*.

B. Change the colon to a comma.

C. Delete *Dear*.

D. Make no change.

The question asks you to think about the rules for writing the salutation of a business letter. Check to see which change, if any, is necessary.

**11.** What editing change, if any, is needed in lines 9–11 ("Although...that.")?

A. Change *suposed* to *supposed*.

B. Place a comma after *hour*.

C. Change *faster* to *fast*.

D. Make no change.

For choice A, you must know the correct spelling of the word. It might help if you sound out the word and break it into syllables. For choice B, you must remember the rules for adding a comma. Does a comma belong at this point in the sentence? And for choice C, you must decide which word to use when comparing one thing with another.

**12.** What editing change, if any, is needed in lines 14–16 ("Since...students.")?
A. Change *September* to *september.*
B. Change the comma after *September* to a colon.
C. Change *accidents* to *accedents.*
D. Make no change.

This question asks you to remember rules of capitalization, punctuation, and spelling. Is any change needed?

**13.** What editing change, if any, is needed in lines 17–18 ("There...Street.")?
A. Change *have* to *has.*
B. Change the comma to a semicolon.
C. Change *almost* to *all most.*
D. Make no change.

For choice A, is the subject of the sentence singular or plural? If it's singular, use the singular form *has*; if it's plural, use the plural form *have.* For choice B, decide if you need a semicolon to correct a run-on sentence. And, for choice C, which is the correct spelling?

**14.** What is the BEST way to combine the sentences in lines 20–21 ("There...work.")?

A. People are driving home from work at those hours.

B. There is also a lot of traffic at those hours, yet some people are driving home from work.

C. Even though there is a lot of traffic at those hours, some people drive home from work at this time.

D. There is also a lot of traffic at those hours because some people are driving home from work.

Think of what both sentences are trying to say. The new sentence must state the same things and be worded clearly. Which choice is the best?

**15.** Which sentence should be omitted because it does NOT support the focus of the letter?

A. line 9 ("This...cross.")

B. lines 12–13 ("Another...Avenues.")

C. lines 16–17 ("One...injuries.")

D. lines 19–20 ("In...school.")

Sometimes writers include sentences that contain unnecessary information. Read each of the choices and decide which sentence does not belong in the letter.

**16.** What editing change, if any, is needed in line 24?

A. Change *truly* to *Truly*.

B. Change *truly* to *truely*.

C. Add a comma after *truly*.

D. Make no change.

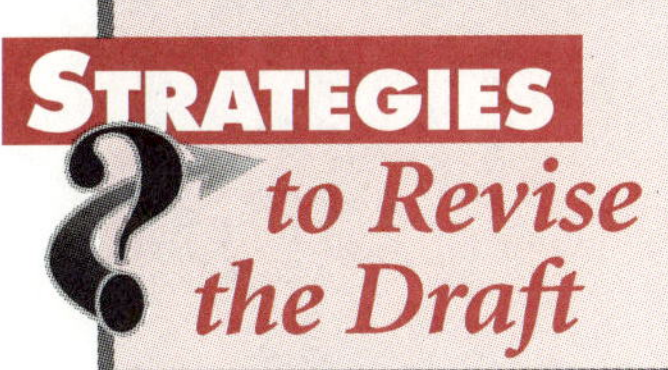


Think about the rules for punctuating, spelling, and capitalizing the closing of a letter.

# Everyday Text

The following passage describes how to make a time capsule. Read the passage and then answer the questions that follow.

**A Time Capsule**

Time capsules are buried in order to show future genirations what your present civilization was like. In 1940, Oglethorpe university in Atlanta, Georgia, buried a number of objects in a time capsule to be dug up in the year 8113. You and your friends can make your very own time capsule.

You'll need an airtight, watertight container—a metal box would be perfect. Next, gather everything you want to put into the capsule. Make sure that anything you choose will say something about the time in which you lived. You might choose articles or advertisements from newspapers and magazines. Or, you might want to include photographs of championship teams or popular movie stars. Some other materials you collect could include the following: words and music of the year's most popular songs, titles of best-selling books, popular movies, and the most-watched television programs, and personal items, such as photographs of your home and family.

Gather all your materials. Place them in the metal box. Seal the box. Put todays date on it and the date it will be opened. Make sure that date is far enough in the future—ten years or more. Then bury the box in the ground. If this is a school or library project indicate in writing the location of the capsule and the "open" date for the folks in the future.

**17.** What editing change, if any, is needed in lines 2–3 ("Time...like.")?

A. Change *are* to *is.*

B. Change *genirations* to *generations.*

C. Change *your* to *you're.*

D. Make no change.

Is there any reason to change the verb from the plural to the singular? Here's a hint: the verb must agree in number with its subject. Next, decide on the correct spelling for choice B. Last, you must decide between a pronoun and a contraction that sound alike. Which one belongs in the sentence?

**18.** What editing change, if any, is needed in lines 3–5 ("In...8113.")?

A. Change *university* to *University.*

B. Delete the comma after *Georgia.*

C. Place a comma after *up.*

D. Make no change.

For this question, you must consider the rules of capitalization and punctuation. What is the rule for capitalizing the name of a particular place? Where do you place commas when separating a city and state in a sentence? And is there any reason to add a comma to the sentence?

**19.** What transition is needed at the beginning of the sentence in lines 7–8 ("You'll...perfect.")?

A. However,

B. Therefore,

C. In addition,

D. First,

What word or phrase best connects this sentence with the previous paragraph? Try each choice and see which best suits the situation.

**20.** What editing change, if any, is needed in lines 11–12 ("Or...stars.")?

A. Place a colon after *include.*

B. Change *teams* to *teems.*

C. Change the period to an exclamation point.

D. Make no change.

For this question, you must think about rules of punctuation and spelling. Does a colon belong after the verb? Which is the correct spelling? Does the sentence indicate enough emotion to warrant an exclamation point? If everything is correct as is, then choice D is the answer.

**21.** What editing change, if any, is needed in lines 12–16 ("Some...family.")?

A. Delete the colon.

B. Change *year's* to *years.*

C. Change the commas after *songs* and *programs* to semicolons.

D. Make no change.

When considering choices A and C, you must remember the rules for adding colons and semicolons to a sentence. For choice B, you must decide if the noun should be possessive or plural.

**22.** What is the BEST way to combine the three sentences in line 17 ("Gather...the box.")?

A. After you've gathered all your materials, place them in the metal box and seal it.

B. Gather all your materials before placing them in the sealed metal box.

C. Before sealing the metal box, place the gathered materials in it.

D. In the metal box, place all of the materials that you've gathered.

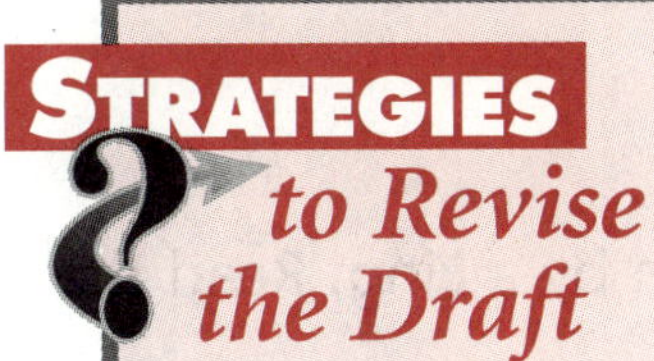


Think of what all three sentences tell you. The new sentence must contain all the important information and be worded clearly. More than one choice might sound correct, but only one presents a clear and logical presentation of the information.

**23.** What editing change, if any, is needed in line 18 ("Put...opened.")?

A. Change *todays* to *today's*.

B. Place a comma after *on it*.

C. Change *opened* to *open*.

D. Make no change.

Should *today* be plural or possessive? Does a comma belong in the sentence? Is there any reason to change the verb tense? If everything is correct, then select choice D.

**24.** What editing change, if any, is needed in lines 20–22 ("If...future.")?

A. Change *library* to *liberty*.

B. Place a comma after *project*.

C. Place a period after *capsule* and change *and* to *And*.

D. Make no change.

This question deals with spelling and punctuation. Decide on the correct spelling of the word. Then look to see if a comma is needed after the introductory clause. Last, decide if this is a run-on sentence that needs to be split into two separate sentences. If everything is correct, make no change.

# CHAPTER Seven

## Guided Practice

Read each passage, answer the questions, and write why you chose those answers.

### Narrative Text

Here is a story about a stingy man who is taught a lesson by a king. Read the story and then answer the questions that follow.

**Bavsi and the King**

Long ago, in the time of King Solomon, there lived a stingy merchant named Bavsi. One day a great famine came and the poor people began to suffer from lack of food. Generous rich men distributed all the contents of their granaries among the starving citizens of jerusalem, but not Bavsi. He put huge wooden bars across the doors of his granaries to keep people out.

King Solomon decided to teach Bavsi a lesson. He sent the merchant an invitation to a feast. Flattered, Bavsi looked forward to the wonderful dinner. On the day of the feast, Bavsi did not eat all day so that he might do the King's savory delights full justise.

Bavsi was led into the room in which King Solomon was waiting. "Sit, Bavsi", said the King, "and let us eat." Bavsi sat, and a servant carried in two bowls of soup like liquid gold, she set one bowl before the King and one before Bavsi. But before the merchant could pick up his spoon, another servant carried the bowl away. With each course, the same thing happened, the food was taken away before Bavsi had time to touch it. By now the merchant was faint with hunger, but he feared saying anything to the King.

Bavsi comforted himself with the thought that he would soon be home, but the King made him stay the night. Bavsi's hunger was gnawing at him. "Why," Bavsi thought, "has the King done this to me? He must want to teach me something." Then Bavsi realized that he had learned the meaning of real hunger.

Bavsi arrived home the next morning. He threw open his granary doors. He distributed his corn to the poor. Never again did he deny food to the hungry.

**1.** What editing change, if any, is needed in lines 3–4 ("One...food.")?

A. Change *famine* to *famin.*

B. Place a comma after *came.*

C. Change *began* to *begin.*

D. Make no change.

The answer is ___________

Reason for choice ________________________________________

________________________________________________________

**2.** What editing change, if any, is needed in lines 4–5 ("Generous...Bavsi.")?

A. Change *their* to *there.*

B. Change *among* to *between.*

C. Change *jerusalem* to *Jerusalem.*

D. Make no change.

The answer is ___________

Reason for choice ________________________________________

________________________________________________________

**3.** What editing change, if any, is needed in lines 9–10 ("On...justise.")?

A. Delete the comma after *feast.*

B. Place a period after *day,* and change *so* to *So.*

C. Change *justise* to *justice.*

D. Make no change.

The answer is ___________

Reason for choice ________________________________________

________________________________________________________

**4.** What editing change, if any, is needed in lines 11–12 ("Sit...eat.")?
A. Delete the comma after *Sit.*
B. Change *Bavsi", said* to *Bavsi," said.*
C. Change *us* to *we.*
D. Make no change.

The answer is ____________

Reason for choice ________________________________________

________________________________________________________

**5.** What editing change, if any, is needed in lines 12–14 ("Bavsi...Bavsi.")?
A. Change *servant* to *servent.*
B. Change the comma after *gold* to a period, and change *she* to *She.*
C. Change *set* to *sat.*
D. Make no change.

The answer is ____________

Reason for choice ________________________________________

________________________________________________________

**6.** What editing change, if any, is needed in lines 15–16 ("With...it.")?
A. Change the comma after *happened* to a colon.
B. Change *was* to *is.*
C. Move *to touch it* between *before* and *Bavsi.*
D. Make no change.

The answer is ____________

Reason for choice ________________________________________

________________________________________________________

**7.** What editing change, if any, is needed in line 20 ("Why...me?")?

A. Delete the comma after *Why*.

B. Change *has* to *Has*.

C. Change the question mark to an exclamation point.

D. Make no change.

The answer is ____________

Reason for choice ________________________________________

____________________________________________________________

**8.** What is the BEST way to combine the three sentences in lines 23–24 ("Bavsi...poor.")?

A. When Bavsi arrived home the next morning, he threw open his granary doors and distributed his corn to the poor.

B. Bavsi distributed his corn to the poor after throwing open his granary doors.

C. Because Bavsi arrived home the next morning, he opened his granary doors to the poor.

D. Bavsi distributed his corn to the poor after arriving home and throwing open his granary doors.

The answer is ____________

Reason for choice ________________________________________

____________________________________________________________

# Informational Text

The following is a short biography of Harriet Tubman. Read the passage and then answer the questions that follow.

**Harriet Tubman**

Harriet Tubman was born a slave in Dorchester County, Maryland about 1821. She escaped to the North around 1849. She later said, “When I crossed that line, I looked at my hands to see if I was the same person. There was such glory over everything. The sun came like gold through the trees, and I felt like I was in heaven. Two other slaves who escaped to freedom were Crispus Attucks and Frederick Douglass.

Wanting to help other slaves escape to freedom Tubman became a “conductor” on the Underground Railroad. This wasn’t a railroad at all, but a chain of homes along an escape route to the North. On the journey North, runaway slaves could safely hide in these homes, called stations. Many stations belonged to quakers or whites who did not believe in slavery, like Susan B. Anthony.

Harriet Tubman made 19 trips on the Underground Railroad. On these trips, she risked her life and endured many hardships. Southerners at one time offerred a reward of $40,000 for her capture, but Tubman was never caught. She may have helped as many as 300 slaves escape. Because of Tubman’s efforts, the slaves called her Moses. Thinking back over her years as a conductor on the Underground Railroad. Tubman said, “I never ran my train off the track or lost a passenger.”

**9.** What editing change, if any, is needed in lines 2–3 ("Harriet...1821.")?

A. Change *County* to *county.*

B. Delete the comma after *County.*

C. Place a comma after *Maryland.*

D. Make no change.

The answer is ____________

Reason for choice ________________________________________

________________________________________________________

**10.** What editing change, if any, is needed in lines 5–6 ("The...heaven.")?

A. Change *through* to *threw.*

B. Delete the comma after *trees.*

C. Place quotation marks after the period.

D. Make no change.

The answer is ____________

Reason for choice ________________________________________

________________________________________________________

**11.** What editing change, if any, is needed in lines 8–9 ("Wanting...Railroad.")?

A. Place a comma after *freedom.*

B. Change *became* to *becomes.*

C. Change *Railroad* to *railroad.*

D. Make no change.

The answer is ____________

Reason for choice ________________________________________

________________________________________________________

**12.** What editing change, if any, is needed in lines 12–13 ("Many...Anthony.")?

A. Change *quakers* to *Quakers*.
B. Change *who* to *whom*
C. Change *believe* to *beleive*.
D. Make no change.

The answer is ____________

Reason for choice ________________________________________

________________________________________________________

**13.** What is the BEST way to combine the sentences in lines 14–15 ("Harriet...hardships.")?

A. After risking her life and enduring many hardships, Harriet Tubman made 19 trips on the Underground Railroad.
B. Because Harriet Tubman risked her life and endured many hardships, she made 19 trips on the Underground Railroad.
C. Although Harriet Tubman made 19 trips on the Underground Railroad, she risked her life and endured many hardships.
D. Harriet Tubman made 19 trips on the Underground Railroad, during which she risked her life and endured many hardships.

The answer is ____________

Reason for choice ________________________________________

________________________________________________________

**14.** What editing change, if any, is needed in lines 16–17 ("Southerners...caught.")?

A. Change *Southerners* to *southerners*.
B. Change *offerred* to *offered*.
C. Delete the comma after *capture*.
D. Make no change.

The answer is ____________

Reason for choice ________________________________________

________________________________________________________

**15.** What editing change, if any, is needed in lines 19–21 ("Thinking...passenger.")?

A. Change the period after *Railroad* to a comma.

B. Delete the comma after *said.*

C. Change *passenger* to *passanger.*

D. Make no change.

The answer is ____________

Reason for choice ________________________________________

________________________________________________________

**16.** Which sentence should be omitted because it does NOT support the focus of the passage?

A. line 3 ("She...1849.")

B. lines 6–7 ("Two...Douglass.")

C. lines 12–13 ("Many...Anthony.")

D. lines 17–18 ("She...escape.")

The answer is ____________

Reason for choice ________________________________________

________________________________________________________

# Persuasive/Argumentative Text

A book report tells what a book is about without telling the whole story. The report also gives the writer's opinions of the book and suggests whether others should read it. Lori wrote the following book report for *The Master Puppeteer*. Read the report. Then answer the questions that follow.

## The Master Puppeteer

*The Master Puppeteer* by Katherine Paterson is an exciting and informative book. This work of historical fiction takes place in eighteenth-century Japan during the Tokugawa period. A poor boy named Jiro becomes an aprentice to Yoshida, the master puppeteer at Osaka's famous puppet theater. Yoshida is a harsh master, especially to his sensitive son, Kinshi. Jiro and Kinshi become fast friends as they live and work together at the Hanaza theater. Jiro also befriends Okada, the elderly blind reciter and playwright.

Things do not go smoothly: Jiro struggles to learn puppetry and the mild Kinshi continually clashes with his stern father. There is also a subplot about a mysterious bandit named Saburo. He steals from the rich to give to the poor. Why are parts of the bandit's disguise found at the Hanaza? What happens when Kinshi defies his father to help the night rovers, starving mobs of rioting peasants who wander the streets? And who is the mastermind behind Saburo? The storys suspense builds and builds as the answers to these questions are masterfully revealed.

Once you start reading, you will find this novel difficult to put down. The compelling drama is swift and exciting. You can learn a great deal about Japan during the Tokugawa period. I especially enjoyed learning about the puppet theater. I once put on a puppet show for my little brother and his friends. The novel provides interesting details about how the puppets were made and manipulated.

**17.** What editing change, if any, is needed in lines 4–6 ("A...theater.")?
   A. Change *aprentice* to *apprentice.*
   B. Delete the comma after *Yoshida.*
   C. Change *Osaka's* to *Osakas.*
   D. Make no change.

The answer is ____________

Reason for choice ________________________________________

________________________________________________________

**18.** What editing change, if any, is needed in lines 7–8 ("Jiro...theater.")?
   A. Change *become* to *became.*
   B. Place a comma after *friends.*
   C. Change *theater* to *Theater.*
   D. Make no change.

The answer is ____________

Reason for choice ________________________________________

________________________________________________________

**19.** What editing change, if any, is needed in lines 10–11 ("Things...father.")?
   A. Change the colon to a comma.
   B. Place a comma after *puppetry.*
   C. Change *continually* to *continualy.*
   D. Make no change.

The answer is ____________

Reason for choice ________________________________________

________________________________________________________

**20.** What is the BEST way to combine the sentences in lines 11–13 ("There...poor.")?

A. A mysterious bandit named Saburo steals from the rich and gives to the poor, and he is the subject of a subplot.

B. There is also a subplot about stealing from the rich to give to the poor.

C. Saburo, a mysterious bandit, steals from the rich to give to the poor.

D. There is also a subplot about a mysterious bandit named Saburo who steals from the rich to give to the poor.

The answer is ____________

Reason for choice ________________________________________

________________________________________________________

**21.** What editing change, if any, is needed in lines 16–17 ("The...revealed.")?

A. Change *storys* to *story's.*

B. Change *are* to *is.*

C. Change *revealed* to *reveeled.*

D. Make no change.

The answer is ____________

Reason for choice ________________________________________

________________________________________________________

**22.** What transition is needed at the beginning of the sentence in lines 19–20 ("You...period.")?

A. First,

B. Therefore,

C. In addition,

D. However,

The answer is ____________

Reason for choice ________________________________________

________________________________________________________

**23.** Which sentence should be omitted because it does NOT support the focus of the passage?

A. lines 3–4 ("This...period.")
B. lines 10–11 ("Things...father.")
C. line 18 ("Once...down.")
D. lines 21–22 ("I...friends.")

The answer is ____________

Reason for choice ________________________________________

________________________________________________________

**24.** Lori wants to add the following sentence to her report: "This book is a must for those who enjoy superb historical fiction." Where would be the BEST place for her to put it?

A. at the beginning of paragraph 1
B. at the end of paragraph 1
C. at the end of paragraph 2
D. at the end of paragraph 3

The answer is ____________

Reason for choice ________________________________________

________________________________________________________

# Independent Practice

Read each passage and answer the questions.

## Passage A

The following passage describes the correct way to look at the sun. Read the passage and then answer the questions that follow.

**How to look at the Sun**

You must never look directly at the sun with your eyes. Not even for a second. It is not even safe to do so if you're wearing sunglasses or looking through smoked glass. If unfiltered sunlight reaches your eyes it can lead to blindness.

The safest way to view the sun is to project it's image through a telescope or binoculars onto a piece of white paper or cardboard. First, mount the telescope or binoculars on a tripod or other rigid support. Remember, do not look through the telescope or binoculars at any time, not even to aim them. Line up the instrument by adjusting its shadow until it is shortest. If using binoculars, keep a dust cap over one of the front lenses to prevent two overlapping images, if using a telescope, keep the finder capped to prevent someone from looking through it by accident.

Center on the sun. Then turn the focusing knob in and out until the image on the cardboard is sharp and clear. You can reduce or enlarge the size of the sun's image by moving the cardboard in and out, but you'll have to refocus the instrument each time the distence changes.

**1.** What revision, if any, is needed in line 1?
A. How to Look at the Sun
B. How To Look at the Sun
C. How To Look At The Sun
D. Make no change.

**2.** What editing change, if any, is needed in lines 2–3 ("You...second.")?
A. Change the period after *eyes* to a colon.
B. Change the period after *eyes* to a semicolon, and change *Not* to *not.*
C. Change the period after *eyes* to a comma, and change *Not* to *not.*
D. Make no change.

**3.** What editing change, if any, is needed in lines 4–5 ("If...blindness.")?
A. Change *sunlight* to *sun light.*
B. Place a comma after *eyes.*
C. Change *lead* to *leed.*
D. Make no change.

**4.** What editing change, if any, is needed in lines 6–7 ("The...cardboard.")?
A. Change *safest* to *safer.*
B. Change *it's* to *its.*
C. Change *piece* to *peace.*
D. Make no change.

**5.** What editing change, if any, is needed in lines 9–10 ("Remember...them.")?
A. Change *through* to *threw.*
B. Change *any time* to *anytime.*
C. Change *aim* to *aime.*
D. Make no change.

**6.** What editing change, if any, is needed in lines 11–14 ("If...accident.")?

A. Delete the comma after *binoculars*.

B. Place a comma after *lenses*.

C. Change the comma after *images* to a semicolon.

D. Make no change.

**7.** What is the BEST way to combine the sentences in lines 15–16 ("Center...clear.")?

A. Once you are centered on the sun, turn the focusing knob in and out until the image on the cardboard is sharp and clear.

B. Turn the focusing knob, centered on the sun, in and out until the image on the cardboard is sharp and clear.

C. Turn the focusing knob in and out after you are centered on the sun.

D. Make the image on the cardboard sharp and clear by centering on the sun.

**8.** What editing change, if any, is needed in lines 16–18 ("You...changes.")?

A. Change *sun's* to *suns*.

B. Delete the comma after *out*.

C. Change *distence* to *distance*.

D. Make no change.

# Passage B

Here is one of Aesop's fables. Read the fable and then answer the questions that follow.

## The Man, His Son, and the Donkey

A man and his son was leading a donkey to market in order to sell it. They chanced upon a traveler who said, "Have you no more sense than to plod along, allowing your donkey to go without a load!" So the man put his son on the donkey, and they continued on their way.

"Young man", said the next person they met, "aren't you ashamed to ride while your poor old father walks?" The man quickly lifted off his son and got on the donkey himself.

Two women passed by, one saying to the other, "Look at that selfish old man, riding while his little boy is forced to follow on foot!" So the man lifted his son and placed him up behind him. People sit on a donkey in the same way they sit on a horse.

The next traveler they met scolded, "I pity that poor animal to carry such a great load. Why, you are better able to carry the donkey than he is to carry both of you." The man then tied the donkey's legs to a pole. They carried it into town. They were staggering under the weight. Everyone there laughed to see such a silly sight. Angered by the laughter, the donkey was dropped on the ground by the man, who grabbed his son by the arm and took off for home. He had learned that a person who tries to please everybody pleases nobody.

**9.** What editing change, if any, is needed in lines 2–3 ("A...it.")?
A. Change *was* to *were.*
B. Place a colon after *leading.*
C. Change *sell* to *cell.*
D. Make no change.

**10.** What editing change, if any, is needed in lines 3–4 ("They...load!")?
A. Change *traveler* to *travelor.*
B. Change *than* to *then.*
C. Change the exclamation point to a question mark.
D. Make no change.

**11.** What editing change, if any, is needed in lines 6–7 ("Young...walks?")?
A. Change *man", said* to *man," said.*
B. Change *aren't* to *Aren't.*
C. Place a comma after *ride.*
D. Make no change.

**12.** What transition is needed at the beginning of the sentence in lines 9–10 ("Two...foot!")?
A. Next,
B. For example,
C. However,
D. Consequently,

**13.** What editing change, if any, is needed in lines 13–14 ("The...load")?
A. Change *met* to *meet.*
B. Place a comma after *animal.*
C. Place quotation marks after *load.*
D. Make no change.

**14.** What is the BEST way to combine the sentences in lines 15–16 ("The...weight.")?

A. The man then tied the donkey's legs to a pole, and they carried it into town, and they were staggering under the weight.

B. After tying the donkey's legs to a pole, they carried it into town.

C. They carried the donkey into town after tying its legs to a pole and staggering under the weight.

D. The man then tied the donkey's legs to a pole and, staggering under the weight, they carried it into town.

**15.** What is the BEST revision for the sentence in lines 17–19 ("Angered...home.")?

A. The man grabbed his son by the arm and took off for home after dropping the donkey on the ground, angered by the laughter.

B. Angered by the laughter, the man dropped the donkey on the ground, grabbed his son by the arm, and took off for home.

C. The donkey, angered by the laughter, was dropped on the ground by the man, who grabbed his son by the arm and took off for home.

D. The son was grabbed by the arm by his father, who dropped the donkey on the ground after being angered by the laughter, and took off for home.

**16.** Which sentence should be omitted because it does NOT support the focus of the passage?

A. lines 4–5 ("So...way.")

B. lines 7–8 ("The...himself.")

C. lines 11–12 ("People...horse.")

D. line 17 ("Everyone...sight.")

# Passage C

The following passage tells how coral reefs are formed. Read the selection and then answer the questions that follow.

## Coral Reefs

Did you know that some rocks can "grow?" The most common type of growing rock is limestone, which grows into huge, thick coral reefs. The coral part is really a small, wormy animal that looks like a minerature sea anemone. They are found in tropical and subtropical waters, at temperatures above 70° and at depths not much below 90 feet.

Why isn't this wormy little animal swept away by ocean waves? The coral discover the art of building construction long before humans did. Coral secrete the mineral calcium carbonate to glue themselves together in sturdy underwater apartments. Some of these structures are called staghorn coral because they resemble antlers. Others that look like a brain are appropriately called brain coral. These are often several feet in diameter. The fancy coral structures remain long after the death of the animals that made them. They provide shelter for other forms of sea life such as fish, crustaceans, and algae.

You may think that a tiny animal can't make all that much rock. The secret is millions of little corals working for thousands of years. They can secrete a great amount of limestone. One of the largest of these structures is the great barrier reef off the east coast of Australia. It's more than 1,200 miles long and all built by coral. Australia is both a continent and an independent country in the southern hemisphere.

**17.** What editing change, if any, is needed in line 2 ("Did...grow?")?

A. Change *know* to *no.*

B. Change *can* to *may.*

C. Move the end quotation marks in front of the question mark.

D. Make no change.

**18.** What editing change, if any, is needed in lines 2–5 ("The...anemone.")?

A. Change *is* to *was.*

B. Change *that* to *who.*

C. Change *minerature* to *miniature.*

D. Make no change.

**19.** What would make the meaning clearer in lines 5–6 ("They...feet.")?

A. Change *They* to *Coral.*

B. Add *in* before *subtropical.*

C. Replace the comma with a colon.

D. Spell out the numbers.

**20.** What editing change, if any, is needed in lines 7–8 ("The...did.")?

A. Change *discover* to *discovered.*

B. Place a comma after *construction.*

C. Change the period to an exclamation point.

D. Make no change.

**21.** What editing change, if any, is needed in lines 11–12 ("Others...coral.")?

A. Change *like* to *as.*

B. Place a comma after a *brain.*

C. Change *appropriately* to *appropriatly.*

D. Make no change.

**22.** What transition is needed at the beginning of the sentence in lines 14–15 ("They...algae")?

A. First,

B. However,

C. Likewise,

D. Consequently,

**23.** What editing change, if any, is needed in lines 18–19 ("One...Australia.")?

A. Change *largest* to *larger.*

B. Change *is* to *are.*

C. Change *great barrier reef* to *Great Barrier Reef.*

D. Make no change.

**24.** Which sentence should be omitted because it does NOT support the focus of the passage?

A. lines 2–4 ("The...reefs.")

B. lines 9–10 ("Coral...apartments.")

C. line 16 ("You...rock.")

D. lines 20–21 ("Australia...hemisphere.")

# Unit 5 Practice Tests

## Introduction

This unit consists of two practice tests. In the first part of each test you will be given a specific situation to write about. The second part of each test includes three passages. Each passage is followed by questions that will require you to use your revising and editing skills. The passages are samples of different types of writing you read about earlier in the book. Use the strategies you learned to help you with your writing and your editing.

# Practice Test A

### Directions for Writing Practice Test A, Part A1

This is Part 1 of the Writing Test. This part is designed to show how well you can write. For this exercise, you are asked to complete a writing task.

Take the time to think about the writing task and how you will organize what you want to say before you begin to write. Make any outline, notes, lists, or organizers, you wish. Only your writing, not your prewriting, will be scored. Do your best to make your writing clear and well organized. Keep in mind the purpose of your writing task as well as your audience.

You may not use a dictionary or any other reference materials during the test. However, you may use the "Writer's Checklist" on page 128, which lists important points for you to remember as you write. If you finish early, go back over your writing using the "Writer's Checklist" to improve what you have written.

Do not go on to Part 2 until you receive further directions.

# Writing Task

## Writing Situation

Many parents of children in your school belong to the Concerned Parents group. This group is worried about the amount of time their children spend watching television. They are considering limiting their children's TV viewing.

## Directions for Writing

Decide how you feel about this issue. Write a letter to the head of the Concerned Parents group expressing your point of view. Include reasons, details, and/or examples that support your opinion. Remember that you want to convince the group that your viewpoint is reasonable.

### Directions for Writing Practice Test A, Part A2

This is Part 2 of the Writing Test. This part consists of three passages in need of editing. Each passage is followed by multiple-choice questions related to the editing of the passage.

Read the entire passage before answering the questions. Mark only one answer for each test item.

# Passage A

*While staying with his aunt and uncle for the summer, Don made friends with their neighbors' son, Jacob. Jacob's family is planning a camping trip and have invited Don to go along. But first he must get his parents' permission. Don wrote the following letter to persuade his parents to let him go on the trip. Read the letter and then answer the questions that follow.*

365 Hillcrest Drive
Sante Fe NM 87501
July 6, 1999

Dear mom and dad,

How are you? Everyone hear is fine, and I'm having a great time. The summer has been wonderful. I have been doing lots of things with my new friend, Jacob. Jacob and his family live next door to Aunt Renee and Uncle Walter. Who have known them for years.

Jacob and his family are planning a weeks camping trip and have invited me along, if you say that it's all right. I'd really love to go. The Jacksons, Jacob's parents, say that I will be good company for him and that I won't be any bother at all. Uncle Walter has agreed to lend me his sleeping bag and any other camping equipment I need. And the trip won't cost much. I need only enough money for souveneers and extra things that I might want to purchase.

The Jacksons are planning to visit the Grand Canyon. They plan to do things like backpacking and taking a mule caravan down the canyon. They also plan to ride the river and go fishing. I know I'd have a great time. Please say that I can go. The Jacksons are leaving on August 10, so I'll need to let them know at least a week before that.

Aunt Renee and Uncle Walter send their love, they say that they would be happy to speak to you about the trip. Please write soon.

Love,
Don

**1.** What editing change, if any, is needed in lines 1–3?
A. Change *Drive* to *drive*.
B. Place a comma after *Santa Fe*.
C. Delete the comma after 6.
D. Make no change.

**2.** What revision, if any, is needed in line 4?
A. Dear Mom And Dad,
B. Dear mom and dad:
C. Dear Mom and Dad,
D. Make no change.

**3.** What editing change, if any, is needed in line 5 ("Everyone...time.")?
A. Change *hear* to *here*.
B. Change *is* to *are*.
C. Delete the comma after *fine*.
D. Make no change.

**4.** What editing change, if any, is needed in lines 7–8 ("Jacob...years.")?
A. Change *live* to *lives*.
B. Change the period after *Walter* to a comma, and change *Who* to *who*.
C. Change *Who* to *Whom*.
D. Make no change.

**5.** What editing change, if any, is needed in lines 9–10 ("Jacob...right.")?
A. Change *weeks* to *week's*.
B. Place a comma after *trip*.
C. Change *it's* to *its*.
D. Make no change.

**6.** What editing change, if any, is needed in lines 14–15 ("I...purchase.")?
A. Change *I need only* to *Only I need*.
B. Change *souveneers* to *souvenirs*.
C. Change the period to an exclamation point.
D. Make no change.

**7.** What is the BEST way to combine the sentences in lines 16–18 ("The...fishing.")?
A. The Jacksons are planning to visit the Grand Canyon and go backpacking and take a mule caravan down the canyon.
B. Planning things like backpacking, taking a mule caravan, riding the river, and fishing, the Jacksons are planning to visit the Grand Canyon.
C. The Grand Canyon is the place the Jacksons are planning to visit, where they will do things like backpacking, riding the river, and fishing.
D. The Jacksons are planning to visit the Grand Canyon and do things like backpacking, taking a mule caravan down the canyon, riding the river, and fishing.

**8.** What editing change, if any, is needed in lines 21–22 ("Aunt...trip.")?
A. Change the comma after *love* to a period, and change *they* to *They*.
B. Place a colon after *say*.
C. Place a comma after *you*.
D. Make no change.

# Passage B

*The following passage is from a handbook on emergency medical care. Read the passage and then answer the questions that follow.*

**Removing an Object from the eye**

A foreign body in the eye, such as a speck of soot or a hair, is very common. If the speck cannot be seen or easily removed, a doctor should be consulted promptly.

A foreign body under the lower lid usually is easily seen and is fairly easy to remove with moistened sterile gauze or cotton. If the object is under the upper lid, it can sometimes be removed by drawing the upper lid down over the lower lid. The flushing and wetting effect of the tears which the irritation produces will tend to make it stick to the lower lid. If the object is not flushed out, turn back the upper lid for inspection. To do this, first grasp the eyelashes gently. Then, with the patient looking down, turn the lid back over a cotton swab. If the speck is seen, wipe it off very gently with a bit of moistened sterile gauze or twisted absorbent cotton. Absorbent cotton has many good uses.

Quite often, an object may be lodged on the cornea of the eye, over the iris. There it may be overlooked because of its dark, matching color. Extreme care should be taken because of the danger of damaging the cornea. Let a doctor handle such a situation. In the meantime, place a sterile eye pad over the eye to help avoid painful and irittating movement. Hold the pad in place with a light bandage or adhesive tape.

The National Society for the Prevention of blindness recommends that specks that cannot be washed out with tears should have medical attention. When it is not possible to obtain medical aid promptly, the above mentioned steps will prove useful.

**9.** What revision, if any, is needed in line 1?

A. Removing an object from the eye

B. Removing An Object From the Eye

C. Removing an Object from the Eye

D. Make no change.

**10.** What editing change, if any, is needed in lines 2–3 ("A…common.")?

A. Change *foreign* to *foriegn*.

B. Change the comma after *eye* to a semicolon.

C. Change *is* to *are*.

D. Make no change.

**11.** What editing change, if any, is needed in lines 5–6 ("A…cotton.")?

A. Place a comma after *seen*.

B. Replace *fairly* with *farely*.

C. Place a colon after *remove*.

D. Make no change.

**12.** What editing change, if any, would make the meaning clearer in lines 8–10 ("The…lid.")?

A. Change *The flushing and wetting effect of the tears* to *The tears' flushing and wetting effect.*

B. Delete *which the irritation produces.*

C. Change *it* to *the object.*

D. Make no change.

**13.** What editing change, if any, is needed in lines 19–21 ("In…movement.")?

A. Delete the comma after *meantime.*

B. Place a comma after *eye.*

C. Change *irittating* to *irritating.*

D. Make no change.

**14.** What editing change, if any, is needed in lines 23–25 ("The…attention.")?

A. Change *blindness* to *Blindness.*

B. Place a colon after *recommends.*

C. Place a comma after *tears.*

D. Make no change.

**15.** What transition should be added to the beginning of the sentence in lines 25–26 ("When…useful.")?

A. For one thing,

B. However,

C. Therefore,

D. For example,

**16.** Which sentence should be omitted because it does not support the focus of the passage?

A. lines 3–4 ("If…promptly.")

B. lines 14–15 ("Absorbent…uses.")

C. lines 18–19 ("Extreme…cornea.")

D. lines 25–26 ("When…useful.")

GO ON

## Passage C

*The following is a true story about a brave doctor. Read the story and then answer the questions that follow.*

### Dr. Ephraim McDowell

In 1799, Dr. Ephraim McDowell returned home to Kentucky after studying medicine in Virginia and scotland. Dr. McDowell soon became famous for his medical knowledge.

One winter night, McDowell was called to examine a patient named Mrs. Crawford. She was in great pain. The doctor soon discovered that the cause of the pain was a growth in her stomach. "She'll die unless I remove it", he told the other doctors who were present.

"Cut her open?" the doctors asked in disbelief. "No one can cut into a person's stomach. You'll kill her!"

McDowell explained everything to Mrs. Crawford. He said that she would suffer great pain while he was operating and might even die. He also explained that she would surely die without the operation. The brave woman nodded her consent.

When McDowell took Mrs. Crawford back to his office, he found that everyone was against him. Even his friends talked of hanging him if he operated, but the doctor thought only of his patient. As he prepared to operate, an angry crowd gathered outside and shouted, "murderer!" A rock came crashing through the window.

McDowell tried to ignore the crowd and Mrs. Crawford prepared herself for the pain. Looking straight ahead, she began to sing an old hymn. When the crowd heard her, they grew silent. As they listened, the strong voice grew weaker and finally stopped.

The operation was a success, less than a month later, Mrs. Crawford went home and lived to a ripe old age. McDowell, however, died several years later of appendicitis. Ironically, he could have been saved if his doctor had known how to operate.

**17.** What editing change, if any, is needed in lines 2–3 ("I…scotland.")?

A. Place a comma after *Kentucky*.
B. Change *medicine* to *medecine.*
C. Change *scotland* to *Scotland.*
D. Make no change.

**18.** What is the BEST way to combine the sentences in lines 5–6 ("One…pain.")?

A. One winter night, McDowell was called to examine a patient named Mrs. Crawford, who was in great pain.
B. McDowell was called to examine a patient named Mrs. Crawford, and she was in great pain.
C. In great pain, McDowell was called to examine a patient named Mrs. Crawford one winter night.
D. Called to examine a patient named Mrs. Crawford, McDowell did so one winter night.

**19.** What editing change, if any, is needed in lines 7–8 ("She'll…present.")?

A. Change *die* to *dye.*
B. Change *it", he* to *it," he.*
C. Change *who* to *whom.*
D. Make no change.

**20.** What editing change, if any, is needed in lines 11–12 ("He…die.")?

A. Put quotation marks before *she* and after *die.*
B. Change *pain* to *pane.*
C. Change the period to an exclamation point.
D. Make no change.

**21.** What transition should be added to the beginning of the sentence in line 13 ("He…operation.")?

A. Consequently,
B. For instance,
C. However,
D. First,

**22.** What editing change, if any, is needed in lines 17–19 ("As…murderer!")?

A. Delete the comma after *operate.*
B. Change *gathered* to *gathers.*
C. Change *murderer* to *Murderer.*
D. Make no change.

**23.** What editing change, if any, is needed in lines 20–21 ("McDowell…pain.")?

A. Change *ignore* to *ignor.*
B. Place a comma after *crowd.*
C. Change *prepared* to *prepares.*
D. Make no change.

**24.** What editing change, if any, is needed in lines 24–25 ("The…age.")?

A. Change the comma after *success* to a colon.
B. Delete the comma after *success.*
C. Place a comma after *home.*
D. Make no change.

GO ON

# Practice Test B

### Directions for Writing Practice Test B, Part B1

This is Part 1 of the Writing Test. This part is designed to show how well you can write. For this exercise, you are asked to complete a writing task.

Take the time to think about the writing task and how you will organize what you want to say before you begin to write. Make any outline, notes, lists, or organizers, you wish. Only your writing, not your prewriting, will be scored. Do your best to make your writing clear and well organized. Keep in mind the purpose of your writing task as well as your audience.

You may not use a dictionary or any other reference materials during the test. However, you may use the "Writer's Checklist" on page 128, which lists important points for you to remember as you write. If you finish early, go back over your writing using the "Writer's Checklist" to improve what you have written.

Do not go on to Part 2 until you receive further directions.

# Writing Task

## Writing Situation

A magazine you read is offering $100 for short articles about personal experiences from its readers. Every month there is a different theme for the articles. This month's articles must be about a humorous experience.

## Directions for Writing

Write an article for the magazine about a humorous personal experience. Include the details and description that will help your readers understand what happened and how you felt about it.

### Directions for Writing Practice Test B, Part B2

This is Part 2 of the Writing Test. This part consists of three passages in need of editing. Each passage is followed by multiple-choice questions related to the editing of the passage.

Read the entire passage before answering the questions. Mark only one answer for each test item.

# Passage A

*The following passage tells about a slave mutiny. Read the passage and then answer the questions that follow.*

**Mutiny Aboard the Amistad**

Joseph Cinque was an African prince who was kidnapped and sold into slavery in Havana Cuba. In 1839, Cinque and fifty-three other African slaves were forced onto a Spanish ship, the *Amistad*. The men who bought the slaves had hired the ship to take them to Puerto Principe in Cuba. One stormy night, Cinque and his fellow Africans carefully planned their escape. The slaves got a hold of some knives carried out a revolt, and took over the ship.

The Africans spared the lives of the two Spanish slave owners, who knew how to steer the ship. Cinque ordered the Spaniards to sail back to Africa. However, the men only pretended they were headed for Cinques homeland. They sailed for New York, because they knew that slavery was still legal in some parts of the United States. The U.S. navy captured the *Amistad* off the coast of Long Island, and Cinque and the other Africans were sent to prison for mutiny and murder.

Two years passed, during which the Africans did not know what would happen to them. In 1841, the case finally came before the U.S. Supreme Court. Former President John Quincy Adams spoke. He spoke on behalf of Joseph Cinque and his men. He argued that the right of every human being was to be free. The court ruled in favor of Cinque and the other Africans. Later that year, they returned to Africa, where Joseph Cinque continued to be a leader among his people. Nelson Mandela is another great African leader who fought for freedom.

**1.** What editing change, if any, is needed in lines 2–3 ("Joseph...Cuba.")?
A. Change *prince* to *Prince.*
B. Change *kidnapped* to *kiddnaped.*
C. Place a comma after *Havana.*
D. Make no change.

**2.** What editing change, if any, is needed in lines 4–6 ("The...Cuba.")?
A. Change *who* to *whom.*
B. Place a comma after *slaves.*
C. Change *Principe* to *principe.*
D. Make no change.

**3.** What editing change, if any, is needed in lines 7–8 ("The...ship.")?
A. Place a comma after *knives.*
B. Change *carried* to *carry.*
C. Change the period to an exclamation point.
D. Make no change.

**4.** What editing change, if any, is needed in lines 11–12 ("However...homeland.")?
A. Change *the men only* to *only the men.*
B. Place a colon after *pretended.*
C. Change *Cinques* to *Cinque's.*
D. Make no change.

**5.** What transition should be added to the beginning of the sentence in lines 12–13 ("They...States.")?
A. For example,
B. Instead,
C. In addition,
D. As a result,

**6.** What editing change, if any, is needed in lines 13–15 ("The...murder.")?
A. Change *navy* to *Navy.*
B. Change the comma after *Island* to a semicolon.
C. Change *were* to *was.*
D. Make no change.

**7.** What is the BEST way to combine the sentences in lines 18–20 ("Former...free.")?
A. On behalf of Joseph Cinque and his men, former President John Quincy Adams spoke.
B. Former President John Quincy Adams spoke on behalf of Joseph Cinque and his men, arguing that the right of every human being was to be free.
C. Arguing that the right of every human being was to be free, Joseph Cinque and his men were defended by former President John Quincy Adams.
D. Former President John Quincy Adams argued that the right of every human being was to be free on behalf of Joseph Cinque and his men.

**8.** Which sentence should be omitted because it does not support the focus of the passage?
A. lines 6–7 ("One...escape.")
B. lines 9–10 ("The...ship.")
C. lines 16–17 ("Two...them.")
D. lines 23–24 ("Nelson...freedom.")

# Passage B

*Keshia was upset when she found out that she was not allowed to wear shorts to school. She wrote the following letter to the principal of her school. Read the letter and then answer the questions that follow.*

Dear Mr. Chavez;

I am writing to ask you to consider allowing the students to wear shorts to school. Enclosed find a petition signed by more than one hundred students who support my proposel.

As you know, we are in the middle of a major heat wave this may. I have taken the inside temperature for two weeks. During this time, the temperature has risen above 90° all but one day and that day it reached 88°. Although some school offices have air-conditioning, the classrooms do not, this makes conditions very uncomfortable.

It is difficult to learn when you have to think about how hot you are. Wearing shorts would help. We would agree not to wear shorts on cool days and not to wear very short shorts or tank tops. I would be happy to meet with you to discuss any other conditions you would require. If students don't adhere to the rules you can forbid them to wear shorts for the following two weeks.

I am requesting that you let students wear the shorts for a trial period of one week. If there are major problems, you could then ban the shorts again. What do you have to lose? Please give us the chance to show you that we can handle this privilege responsibly.

Yours truly,

Keshia Brown

**9.** What revision, if any, is needed in line 1?

A. Dear Mr. Chavez:
B. Dear Mr. Chavez,
C. Dear Mr. Chavez.
D. Make no change.

**10.** What editing change, if any, is needed in lines 3–4 ("Enclosed...proposel.")?

A. Change *who* to *whom.*
B. Change *support* to *supports.*
C. Change *proposel* to *proposal.*
D. Make no change.

**11.** What editing change, if any, is needed in line 5 ("As...may.")?

A. Delete the comma after *know.*
B. Change *major* to *majer.*
C. Change *may* to *May.*
D. Make no change.

**12.** What editing change, if any, is needed in lines 6–8 ("During...88°.")?

A. Delete the comma after *time.*
B. Change *temperature* to *temperture.*
C. Place a comma after *one day.*
D. Make no change.

**13.** What editing change, if any, is needed in lines 8–9 ("Although...uncomfortable.")?

A. Change *have* to *had.*
B. Change the comma after *not* to a period, and change *this* to *This.*
C. Change *uncomfortable* to *uncomfortible.*
D. Make no change.

**14.** What editing change, if any, is needed in lines 14–15 ("If...weeks.")?

A. Change *students* to *student's.*
B. Place a comma after *rules.*
C. Change *forbid* to *forbade.*
D. Make no change.

**15.** What editing change, if any, is needed in lines 18–19 ("Please...responsibly.")?

A. Place a comma after *you.*
B. Change *we* to *us.*
C. Change *privilege* to *privledge.*
D. Make no change.

**16.** Keshia wants to add the following sentence to her letter: "Thank you for your consideration." Where would be the BEST place for her to put it?

A. At the end of paragraph 1.
B. At the end of paragraph 2.
C. At the end of paragraph 3.
D. As a separate paragraph after paragraph 4.

# Passage C

*This passage tells how to do an experiment. Read the passage and then answer the questions that follow.*

**What Happens When Air Is Heated**

You can do an experiment to find out what happens when air is heated. The first thing to do is gather all the necessary materials. Gathering materials is usually the first step in any experiment. You'll need the following; two wooden boards about 3 feet long, two chairs, two small milk cartons, a pair of scissors or a knife, string, and a small electric lamp.

Place one of the boards between the two chairs, which should be about a foot apart. Then, balance the other board over the middle of the first one to form a cross.

Cut off the tops of the two milk cartons and punch holes in the bottoms. Put string through the holes to make handles for each carton. Tie the string so that the handles are about 6 to10 inches long and then cut off any excess string. Using the handle, hang a carton from each end of the second board so that they balance. Then turn on the electric lamp, put it under one of the cartons.

Carefully observe the cartons. You will notice that the carton being heated moves up. While the other carton moves down. This shows that heating the carton makes the air inside lighter, causing the carton to rise. This same principal makes hot-air balloons rise into the sky.

**17.** What revision, if any, is needed in line 1?

A. What Happens when Air is Heated
B. What Happens When air is Heated
C. What Happens When Air Is Heated?
D. Make no change.

**18.** What editing change, if any, is needed in lines 4–7 ("You'll...lamp.")?

A. Change the semicolon to a colon.
B. Change *scissors* to *scizzors.*
C. Delete the comma after *string.*
D. Make no change.

**19.** What transition should be added to the beginning of the sentence in lines 8–9 ("Place...apart.")?

A. However,
B. In addition,
C. For example,
D. First,

**20.** What editing change, if any, is needed in lines 13–14 ("Tie...string.")?

A. Change *are* to *were.*
B. Place a comma after *long.*
C. Change *excess* to *access.*
D. Make no change.

**21.** What editing change, if any, is needed in lines 15–16 ("Then...cartons.")?

A. Change *Then* to *Than.*
B. Add *and* after the comma.
C. Change *cartons* to *carton's.*
D. Make no change.

**22.** What editing change, if any, is needed in lines 17–18 ("You...down.")?

A. Change the period after *up* to a comma, and change *While* to *while.*
B. Change the period after *up* to a colon, and change *While* to *while.*
C. Change the period after *up* to a semicolon, and change *While* to *while.*
D. Make no change.

**23.** What editing change, if any, is needed in line 20 ("This...sky.")?

A. Change *principal* to *principle.*
B. Change *makes* to *made.*
C. Change *rise* to *raise.*
D. Make no change.

**24.** Which sentence should be omitted because it does not support the focus of the passage?

A. lines 2–3 ("You...heated.")
B. line 4 ("Gathering...experiment.")
C. lines 11–12 ("Cut...bottoms.")
D. lines 18–20 ("This...rise.")

# Writer's Checklist

## Important Points to Remember as You Write and Critically Read to Revise/Edit Your Writing

### Content/Organization

1. Focus on your purpose for writing and on your audience. Convince your audience that your point of view, solution, or causes and/or effects are reasonable.
2. Support your point of view, solution, or causes and/or effects with details and evidence.
3. Put your ideas in the order that best communicates what you are trying to say.

### Sentence Construction

4. Use clear and varied sentences.

### Usage

5. Use words correctly.

### Mechanics

6. Capitalize, spell, and punctuate correctly.
7. Write neatly.